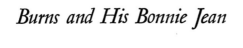

Burns and His Bonnie Jean

Burns and His Bonnie Jean

The Romance of Robert Burns and Jean Armour

by

Yvonne Helen Stevenson

Gray's Publishing Ltd.

SIDNEY, BRITISH COLUMBIA, CANADA

Printed by Evergreen Press Limited
Vancouver, B.C., Canada

AUTHOR'S NOTE

The romance of Robert Burns and Jean Armour has been comparatively neglected by Burns biographers at large and confusion exists as to the relative major and minor importance of the poet's reputed love affairs. Urged by prominent Burns devotees, I have placed on record in the following pages the story of the Burns-Armour *cause celebre* as the facts were known in the family circle of my Armour forebears.

For twentieth century Burns students there is a wealth of well-documented source material to be found in the early Burns biographies of Heron, Currie, Lockhart, Hately Waddell, Chambers, Hamilton Paul, Cunningham and others; and in the more recent biographies of the late Prof. J. DeLancey Ferguson, Hilton Brown, David Daiches, Hans Hecht (translated by Jane Lymburn), Dr. Franklyn B. Snyder, Catherine Carswell and Maurice Lindsay. To all of these authorities I acknowledge a deep debt of gratitude for their competent research. Particularly am I indebted to the work of the late Prof. J. DeLancey Ferguson for his masterly editing of existing Burns letters in the hands of private collectors, libraries and museums resulting in the publication of his *The Letters of Robert Burns* by Oxford Clarendon Press in 1931.

In an intimately personal sense I wish to acknowledge the generous assistance of my kinsman Hugh Hood of Glasgow—also an Armour descendant —and many other relatives each of whom contributed a facet or two to the mosaic of this book; and to Thomas W. Dalgleish, O.B.E., F.S.F., prominent Burnsian, who encouraged its completion and graciously consented to contribute a Foreword. In addition, grateful thanks are due to Maynard Gertler, well-known Montreal editor, for guidance and counsel in preparation of the manuscript and to Mary Gibbs of Sidney for final revisions.

Finally, apologies are due to the shade of Burns himself for the liberties I have taken in substituting here and there an Anglo-Saxon word for a Doric one to make his meaning clearer. Even in the poet's own day, reviewers of the first edition of his *Poems* expressed a fear that, due to the dialect he employed, appeal of his work would be limited as use of the Doric tongue had waned after the Union of the Crowns in 1707. Wrote Henry Mackenzie, editor of *The Lounger,* soon after the *Poems* appeared: "Even in Scotland, the provincial dialect which the poets Ramsay and Burns have used is now read with a difficulty which greatly damps the pleasure of the reader; in England, it cannot be read at all without such constant reference to a glossary as nearly to destroy the pleasure." Dr. John Moore of Glasgow, then living in London, constantly urged Burns to compose in English to ensure a wider market for his work but to all such persuasions Burns turned a deaf ear, declaring to Thomson who had invited him to contribute to his *Collection of Scottish Melodies*: "These English songs gravel me to death! If you are for English verses, there is, on my part, an end of the matter . . . I can only hope to please myself in being allowed at least a sprinkling of my native tongue."

Were Burns alive today, however, he might take a very different view of the matter and might even applaud an effort to bring his incomparable songs and poems before a much wider audience.

Yvonne Helen Stevenson

Victoria, B.C.

September, 1967

FOREWORD

It is with pride and pleasure I introduce to Burns lovers the world o'er Yvonne Helen Stevenson's book *Burns and His Bonnie Jean*. I had the pleasure of meeting the author in Victoria, British Columbia, during my world tour in 1966.

A direct descendant of the Armour family of Mauchline in Ayrshire, Miss Stevenson presents the story of the romance of Robert Burns and Jean Armour. Her book will be read with relish by Burns lovers. It mirrors the viewpoint and forebodings of the parents of Bonnie Jean, the girl who married Scotland's famous poet. In the words of William MacFarlane, an outstanding Burnsian in the village of Mauchline, "I know of no other person who knows more about the Armour family than Miss Stevenson."

I have read Miss Stevenson's book with pleasure and am sure this new addition to Burnsian literature will meet with warm acceptance. It has been compiled with great care by an accomplished and competent author.

During my tour of Canada, the U.S.A., New Zealand and Australia I was privileged to meet many enthusiastic Burnsians and I am confident this new book will win world-wide circulation.

I am delighted to be associated with its publication and I recommend *Burns and His Bonnie Jean* as an outstanding link with our National Bard.

Thos. W. Dalgleish, O.B.E., F.S.F.,
Hon. Secretary and Treasurer
The Burns Federation,
Kilmarnock, Ayrshire

Prologue

I have a favourite seat under the copper beeches in Beacon Hill Park in Victoria, capital city of British Columbia. It is close to the granite drinking fountain that supports a small bronze effigy of Burns and Highland Mary. On its plinth is engraved a quotation from a poem once written by Burns:

> The golden hours on angel-wings
> Flew o'er me and my dearie,
> For dear to me as light and life
> Was my sweet Highland Mary.

But so many women were "dear as light and life" to Robert Burns, it seems, and tourists who view the monument are usually puzzled.

"Her name was Mary Campbell," volunteers the man in the faded panama hat. "They exchanged bibles when they parted." His voice trails away thinly. He is uncertain about the rest of their story.

"Didn't they ever get married?" enquires a rosy-cheeked teen-ager as she tussles with her camera. The man in the panama hat looks hopefully round at his neighbours for an answer but nobody seems to have it.

The crowd thins. The stately cruising swans trumpet softly on the gleaming lake near the Rose Gardens and I sit on dreaming of Burns and his true love Jean Armour and resolve to tell the story of their poignant love as it was related in the intimate family circle of my eighteenth century Armour forebears. For Jean Armour is obviously the forgotten woman.

Yvonne Helen Stevenson

> I see thee dancing o'er the green
> Thy waist sae jimp, thy limbs sae clean,
> Thy tempting lips, thy roguish een —
>   By Heaven and Earth I love thee!
>
> By night, by day, a-field, at hame,
> The thoughts o' thee my breast inflame,
> And ay I muse and sing thy name —
>   I only live to love thee.
>
> Tho' I were doom'd to wander on,
> Beyond the sea, beyond the sun,
> Till my last weary sand was run,
>   Till then — and then — I'd love thee!
>   . . . Burns

For my sister Aileen

On a stormy winter day in the year 1784 a handsome young farmer slipped into Poosie Nancie's tavern by a back door and ordered a steaming whisky toddy. At his heels frisked a mongrel dog, its eye primed for canine mischief. Its crudely-fashioned brass collar, secured by a leather thong, bore the inscription *Poet Burns,* a conceit that earned its master amused smiles in his new parish. Robert seldom ventured abroad without the companionable Luath and meant to immortalize his dog in a poem that would limn two canines—one the pet of a rich man, the other a ploughman's tyke—sitting down together by the roadside to compare their social status. Luath's portrait was already simmering in his mind:

> . . . He was a ploughman's collie,
> A rhyming, ranting, raving billie
> Wha for his frien' and comrade had him,
> An' in his freaks had Luath ca'd him
> After some dog in Highland song,
> Was made lang syne—Lord knows how lang.
>
> He was a gash an' faithfu' tyke
> As ever lap a sheugh or dike;
> His honest, sonsie, stripéd face
> Ay gat him friends in ilka place;
> His breast was white, his touzie back
> Weel clad wi' coat o' glossy black;
> His gawcie tail, wi' upward curl
> Hung owre his hurdies wi' a swirl . . .

Interrupting his reveries, Poosie Nancie set the steaming beverage before her unfamiliar patron and, wiping her hands on her voluminous apron and curtseying respectfully after the manner of all good alewives, enquired his name. He was the new tenant of Mossgiel farm he told her—and who did not know lawyer Hamilton's long vacant steading a mile or so from the village—and he had come with his recently widowed mother, Agnes Burns and his younger brothers and sisters to farm the 119-acre property.

Worn out before his time by an endless struggle to make ends meet and "far gone in a consumption" his father, William Burns, had died a few months previously at Lochlea farm in the neighbouring parish of Tarbolton, leaving Robert and his younger brother Gilbert to shoulder the family responsibilities as best they could. His financial affairs had long been precarious and legal proceedings had been launched against him by a callous landlord —described in Robert's poem *The Twa Dogs* in which the rich man's dog was to declaim:

> I've noticed on our Laird's court-day,
> And mony a time my heart's been wae,
> Poor tenant bodies, scant o' cash,
> How they must thole a factor's snash;
> He'll stamp an' threaten, curse and swear
> He'll apprehend them, seize their gear;
> While they must stan' wi' aspect humble
> An' hear it a' and fear an' tremble . . .

Anticipating their father's demise, his eldest sons had looked around for another farm on which they could make a fresh start and, learning that Gavin Hamilton, a local lawyer, wished to find a tenant for the long fallow farm he had held on lease from a titled landowner, they had eagerly signed a lease for Mossgiel at a rental of £90 per annum and, because its soil— long starved for fertilizer—was in extremely poor condition Hamilton promised to be lenient in the matter of rent payment until the family got on its feet financially. It had been the intention of Hamilton to establish a dairy depot at Mossgiel to serve the needs of customers in distant urban centers and the farm was to afford a vacation retreat for city relatives who longed for a breath of fresh country air during oppressive summer weather. But Hamilton's ambitious plans had been suddenly abandoned. Whether he had run out of money to further them or whether, with competent agrarian advice, he had been persuaded that the soil of Mossgiel was unlikely to support his dairy herds is not known for lawyer Hamilton was a shrewd and tight-lipped man. What is known, however, is that the urgent necessities of the Burns family of Tarbolton provided an ideal solution for Hamilton's quandaries and little had been said at the signing of the lease about the superhuman effort that would be needed to bring Mossgiel into profitable production. All might be well if the seasons were kind but sea-girt Ayrshire was frequently lashed by sudden storms and at times early frosts brought disaster to optimistic farmers.

The location of Mossgiel delighted socially-inclined Robert. The farm stood on the crest of a windswept ridge overlooking the picturesque valleys of the Ayr and Cessnock rivers and was situated an easy mile's walk or pony trot from the village of Mauchline which was full of lively, well-dressed girls and boasted a popular ballroom, a well-patronized Singing School and numerous Fairs that encouraged enjoyable social intercourse. Like many rural hamlets of its kind in eighteenth century Scotland, the village of

Mauchline clustered intimately round the "Castle" and the Kirk. The "Castle" was a crumbling, lichened, bat-infested edifice—all that remained of an ancient monastery established in the village by the monks of Melrose during the twelfth century and at the time the Burns family came to live in the parish, it served as a popular rendezvous for young lovers anxious to elude the watchful eye of Kirk Session inquisitors.

The Kirk — "as ugly a lump of consecrated stone as ever encumbered the earth" according to a contemporary historian — had been erected by the monks in 1165. It had a pedigree and a fascinating history. It had witnessed all the stir of the Reformation and had been used down the centuries for both Catholic and Protestant services. In the year 1784, when the Burns family moved into the parish and began to worship there, it still boasted its humiliating cutty stool upon which parish sinners were arraigned for public rebuke on three successive Sundays. Its ancient flat-toned bell, swinging high in the belfry, still proclaimed the inexorable authority of a watchful Kirk Session. The interior of the church was crowded with tiny galleries or "lofts", each approached by a separate stairway and allotted to families of the gentry by a system of social preferment. In an area under the Common Loft for ordinary worshippers, a school was held daily for the village young and, learning that James Smith, a local Casanova, boasted openly of his amorous success with certain flighty matrons in the town, Robert set to work to compose a rib-tickling *Epitaph* describing the trek of Mauchline's young across the kirkyard to the school:

> Lament him, Mauchline husbands a',
>   He often did assist ye;
> For had ye stay'd whole weeks awa'
>   Your wives they ne'er had missed ye.
>
> Ye Mauchline bairns, as on ye pass
>   To school in bands together,
> O, tread ye lightly on his grass
>   Perhaps he was your father.

Circulated privately in manuscript in some of the local taverns that ringed the kirkyard, Robert's *Epitaph* was acclaimed with a roar of alcoholic glee accompanied by a rousing thumping of ale stoups on the bare wooden tables. Here was a man who was likely to inject enlivening mirth into the dull routine of kirk-dominated life in Mauchline town.

Robert's first appearance in the village created interest and speculation. He was, by all counts, an arresting figure of a man. He wrapped his home-spun woollen plaid — the colour of dead leaves — in a somewhat dashing manner around broad and sinewy shoulders that were stooped from long association with the plough. And, in an age when country farmers wore their hair loose, he tied his jet-black locks at the nape of the neck after a fashion prevailing among the rakish young bloods of Edinburgh. His com-

3

plexion was dark and swarthy, his eyes large and luminous and the corners of his mouth curled somewhat scornfully, it seemed. He was five foot ten and carried himself with a slightly theatrical swagger. His age, people guessed, was about twenty-five and, meeting him for the first time, Mauchline townsfolk invariably turned for another look at him. He was the most interesting "incomer" who had come among them for many a long day.

With him from his former parish he had brought a reputation for "daffin' wi' the lassies" and fathers of marriageable girls had sounded a warning tocsin to them and their mothers. In his early days in Tarbolton he had been dubbed "a clever young scamp with a good deal to say for himself" and the graybeards had declared that they "suspected his motives." At outs with the Kirk Session, he had been in the habit of lounging on horseback at the kirkyard gates on Sundays to tilt with departing members of the congregation on moot points of orthodoxy. His effrontery had been deeply resented by the Kirk Session which had held several meetings to discuss his heterodoxy. He had been the prime organizer of a highly suspect Bachelors' Club that met regularly in John Richards's home in the village and it had been reliably reported that he had composed a number of bawdy songs and ballads for the titivation of his graceless boon companions. A copy of one of the songs had fallen into the hands of a scandalized Elder. Its title was *No Churchman am I* and the last line of each stanza proclaimed: "A big-bellied bottle's a cure for a' care!" Moreover, it was reported that young Burns had laid sacrilegious hands upon the First and Ninetieth Psalms of David and "paraphrased" them — a shocking example of levity! Today, however, when the once closely-guarded Rules and Regulations of the Tarbolton Bachelors' Club are no longer a secret to investigators, it would appear that the anxieties of the Kirk were groundless. Membership in the Club was restricted to "not more than sixteen members" all of whom were required to be "the professed lover of one or more of the Fair Sex." Alcoholic indulgence was strictly limited — due no doubt to the general penury of its young members and a single toast only was raised to the health of "The Lassies." Section sixteen of the by-laws of the Club prohibited "all swearing and profane language and particularly all obscene and indecent conversation" and members were duly sworn "not to reveal any of the speeches or affairs of its members" in order to avoid ridicule. Spirited debates were held regularly on topics of paramount interest to ambitious young farmers anxious to improve their future prospects in life and such topics were earnestly harangued:

> Suppose a young man, bred a farmer, but without any fortune, has it in his power to marry either of two girls: the one, a girl of large fortune but neither handsome in appearance nor agreeable in conversation, but who can manage the household affairs of a farm well enough — the other a girl every way agreeable in person, conversation and behaviour but without any fortune. Which of them shall he choose?

It is not difficult to guess that romantic-minded Robert would plump for the lass who was "agreeable in person, conversation and behaviour" and that his younger brother Gilbert would have an eye for the girl who lacked these attributes but had "a large fortune." Later on, in a letter to Dr. John Moore, Robert was to concede frankly that Gilbert "wanted my hair-brained imagination as well as my social and amorous madness" and to confess that, at this particular time: "far beyond all other impulses of my heart, was *un penchant à l'adorable moitié du genre humain*. My heart was completely tinder and was eternally lighted up by some goddess or other. . . ."
Among other topics debated were:

> Whether do we derive more happiness from Love or Friendship?

and

> Whether is a young man of the lower ranks of life likeliest to be happy who has got a good education and his mind well-informed; or he who has just the education and information of those around him?

Here, we are certain, young Robert would be able to argue convincingly for, from his earliest days — commencing at the age of seven years — his father, William Burns, had seen to it that his two eldest sons should receive the best possible education he could afford that was commensurate with rural educational standards of the day. And in this he was like many another Scots farmer who made sacrifices that his sons should be well-equipped educationally to meet the demands of adult life. When young, Robert and Gilbert had attended a tiny school in the parish of Alloway, a stone's throw from the straw-thatched, white clay cottage in which they had been born. And, later on, under the tutelage of a young schoolmaster named John Murdoch who resided alternately on the farms of the parents of his young pupils, the two boys had made excellent progress.

A closer examination of the Constitution and Rules of the Tarbolton Club discloses the guiding hand of young Burns whose passion for democracy and brotherly love were soon to find scope in his adult Masonic associations:

> Every man proper for a member of this Society must have a frank, honest, open heart; above anything dirty or mean. No haughty, self-conceited person who looks upon himself as superior to the rest of the Club — and especially no mean-spirited worldly mortal whose only will is to heap up money — shall upon any pretext whatever be admitted. In short, the proper person for this Society is: a cheerful, honest-hearted lad who, if he has a friend that is true and a mistress that is kind and as much wealth as genteely to make both ends meet, is just as happy as this world can make him.

Unguessed by young Robert at this particular time, he was soon to find, in the adjoining parish of Mauchline, not many years later, a "friend that was true and a mistress that was kind" in the person of Jean Armour, the

5

vivacious young daughter of a prosperous contractor and master mason who was to become "the ruling passion of his life" according to an early biographer, and his meeting with Bonnie Jean was "an event which coloured all his future life imparting to it its brightest lights and its darkest shadows" according to another.

In his autobiographical letter to Dr. John Moore a few years later, Robert was to give a graphic account of his early days at Lochlea farm in the parish of Tarbolton; of his adolescent love affairs in which he was "sometimes received with favour and sometimes mortified with a repulse;" of his father's heartrending encounters with "the hell hounds that growl in the kennels of justice" and of his own efforts to improve his situation by learning the arts of flax-growing and, to enhance his social status, attendance at a dancing school — to which his sober-minded father strenuously objected. He also mentioned his early efforts to "commit the sin of rhyme" and confessed that, at this particular time pride and passion were his besetting sins due to the poverty of his family and his passionate desire for romance. He had been "repulsed" by a respectable young woman named Allison Begbie to whom he had written pompous but hopeful love letters, only to be told by the delectable Allison that she was "sorry but she was promised to another" and she had wished him "all kinds of happiness." He had been snubbed by a local lass named Isabella Steven who gave herself airs because her father owned a few acres of peat-bog in the neighbourhood and on the head of the hoity-toity "Tibbie" he let loose a scathing indictment:

> Yestreen I met you on the moor;
> Ye spak' not but gaed by like stoure: (chaff)
> Ye geck at me because I'm poor
> But deuce a hair care I!
>
> When comin' hame on Sunday last,
> Upon the road as I cam' past
> Ye snuft an' gae your head a cast
> But, trowth, I care na by.
>
> I doubt na, lass, but ye may think
> Because ye hae the name o' clink
> That ye can please me in a wink
> Whene'er ye like to try,
>
> But sorrow tak' him that's sae mean
> Altho' his purse o' coin were clean,
> Wha follows ony saucy quean
> That looks sae proud an' high. . . .
>
> But, Tibbie, lass, tak' my advice,
> Your daddie's gear mak's ye sae nice;
> The deil a ane wad speir your price
> Were ye as poor as I. . . .

and he released a final withering blast indicating his interest in a less haughty and more accessible lassie:

6

There lives a lass beside yon park
I'd rather hae her in her sark   (shirt)
Than you wi' a' your thousand mark
That makes you look sae high!

But the agonies and ecstacies of adolescent love affairs that pricked the skin of sensitive Robert were soon to end and the family move to Mauchline opened up a new chapter for "Venus's barter" — Robert's own soubriquet for romantic bargaining.

CHAPTER 2

With him, when he moved to the farm of Mossgiel, Robert brought the Commonplace Book he had commenced in Tarbolton to record his "own private story, likewise my amours, my rambles, the smiles and frowns of fortune on my bardship, my poems and fragments that must never see the light." Titled *Hints, Songs and Scraps of Poetry,* etc. it was an introspective Pool of Marah reflecting "how a ploughman, little indebted to scholastic education and bred at a plough-tail and following a rustic way of life, thinks and feels under the pressures of love, ambition, anxiety, grief, with the like cares and passions which operate pretty much alike in all species however diversified by the manners and modes of life." Taking himself very seriously at this particular time, he declared in its premise that he intended to make its pages his "confidant" and to "sketch every character that in any way struck me to the best of my observation, with complete justice." Some of his early entries were delightfully naive. He had been "led into a thousand weaknesses and follies by love," he wrote, but, "notwithstanding all that has been said against it respecting the folly and weakness it leads a young, inexperienced mind into, I think it in great measure deserves the highest encomiums that have been passed upon it. If anything on earth deserves the name of rapture or transport, it is the feelings of green eighteen in the company of the mistress of his heart when she repays him with an equal return of affection." By the time he arrived in Mauchline, however, his outlook on adolescent love affairs had undergone a radical change and he was less vulnerable to idle romancing though his eye was still primed for pleasurable new conquests and one of the first entries in his Commonplace Book after settling down at Mossgiel reflected a new facet in his "private story:"

> When first I came to Stewart Kyle
> My mind it wasna' steady;
> Where'er I gaed, where'er I rade
> A sweetheart still I had ay;
> But when I came roun' by Mauchline town

Not dreadin' ony body
My heart was caught afore I thought
And by a Mauchline lady.

The mysterious little stanza was soon followed by a rapturous description of the Mauchline lady's graces:

My girl she's airy, she's buxom and gay
Her breath is as sweet as the blossoms in May;
A touch of her lips it ravishes quite;
I never am happy when out of her sight.
She's always good-natur'd, good humour'd and free
She dances, she glances, she smiles upon me.

Jean Armour, daughter of a Mauchline master mason, was the subject of these rhapsodies. Born on February 26th, 1765, she was seven years younger that Robert and when Robert first made her acquaintance she was the toast of the taverns in the town. She was the second child of James and Mary Armour who lived in a neat white clay, straw-thatched cottage in the Cowgate not far from the old "Castle" and the Parish Church. James Armour was a man of some standing in the shire. He had contracted for and erected Dumfries House, country residence of the Marquis of Bute, near Old Cumnock; Skeldon House on the river Doon; and many of the arched stone bridges that spanned the teeming small rivers of rural Ayrshire. The services of his young apprentices — among them his own son Adam — were in constant demand for the repair of crumbling stone dikes, shifting roof-thatch and storm-toppled chimneys and for the hewing of headstones in country kirkyards. A highly respected Freemason and a pillar of the Church — his advice frequently sought by the Kirk Session on parochial matters that required tactful handling — he was a generous contributor to the parish poor-boxes and he was a welcome visitor in the homes of the local gentry with whom he was on first-name terms. Like many a successful, self-made man, however, Mason Armour acquired enemies who dubbed him "a wee bit mason, fond o' a dram and addicted to snuff." But in an age when the convivial dram at the inn often cemented a rewarding business deal and the exchange of a friendly pinch of snuff was common enough coinage, it would seem that the denigration of Armour was the sour fruit of envy and jealousy. The rumble of the carriage-wheels of the gentry's conveyances on the cobblestones of the Cowgate outside mason Armour's home and the cordial reception he received in the wayside inns, told a more realistic story.

His eldest daughter Jean was a bewitching and vivacious brunette in her late teens when Robert first arrived in the parish. Tall and graceful, she had "a most enticing figure" according to her contemporaries and her witty, saucy, provocative tongue enchanted the sober-minded young farmers who hoped to court her and — such was her father's reputation for severity — knocked timidly at the Armour door. She possessed a charming soprano voice, well-trained in the Mauchline Singing School in an age when solo and group-singing was a social grace and, born under the terpsichorean sign of Pisces, was light as thistledown on her feet and the most popular dancing partner in the Penny Reels held weekly in Hugh Morton's ballroom in the village. While other girls waited forlornly in the street outside in the "pitiful market" for a partner to escort them on to the dance floor, bonnie Jean was usually already there, her merry laughter rising high above the scraping of the fiddler's bow. A born coquette, she flaunted a scarlet riband in her luxuriant dark hair that was fragrant after rinsing in a lotion made with hawthorn buds gathered in May and Robert confided to his landlord, Gavin Hamilton, that she was "a sweet young handsome quean" and "a delicious armful."

The legend of his first meeting with mason Armour's daughter has been often debated by Burns "experts," those indefatigable diggers in the compost heap of existing Burnsiana. The truth of the matter is now only of academic interest to the Burns student and the facts are hard to come by now. Twentieth century Armour descendants accept the version related by Jean herself in later years when there was no need for subterfuge and evasion. And there is the witness of Jean's younger sister Nellie who was with her on what the Armour family came to describe as "the beginning of that unfortunate affair." Nellie Armour, it appears, never forgave Burns for her sister's seduction and, in the years that lay ahead, refused to acknowledge him as a brother-in-law when they were obliged to count him as a member of the intimate family circle and later on, when she had a home of her own, refused to have his portrait on display or a copy of his famous *Poems* in her library. And in this she was a true Armour.

On a lovely April morning, related Jean many years later, she had gone with Nellie to the village bleaching-green near the old Castle to spread the family washing on the grass for whitening in the sunlight. Weary after a strenuous morning at the washtub, the two girls had sat down to rest awhile under a lofty sheltering elm tree that was clamorous with nesting rooks. A sudden gust of wind ruffled the linens on the grass alerting a mischievous little dog frisking at the heels of its master who was approaching from the distance. In the twinkling of an eye the dog broke heel and, with incredibly dirty feet, was soon trampling rapturously over the snowy washing. Enraged beyond endurance, Jean picked up a handful of stones and flung them savagely at the dog. Its yelp of pain and surprise brought its master hastily to Jean's side. The blaze in his eyes matched the fire in her own. Bearing down upon her angrily, he was rocked back on his heels by her fresh young beauty. Her cheeks flamed scarlet and her jet black eyes sparkled dangerously. He noticed that she wore a loose short-sleeved print jacket and that her kilted petticoat was pinned high above a pair of rosy, pretty knees. He approached her more diffidently, his bonnet in his hand, for the harsh words he had intended to fling at her had died stillborn in his throat.

10

"Lassie," he began haltingly, his eyes assessing her enticing figure and her sturdy, shapely limbs, "if ye had ony respect for Poet Burns ye would not be throwing stones at his poor wee dog!" As she had soon suspected, he was Robert Burns, the new tenant of Mossgiel, who had come recently to the parish of Mauchline and he was on his way to visit his landlord Gavin Hamilton at the Castle near the bleaching-green. In no mood for banter, however, Jean had turned on him angrily, her arms akimbo on her hips like any infuriated Gallowgait fishwife. "I have no respect for Poet Burns," she informed him acidly, "nor has anybody else in the town that I've heard tell of," she assured him for good measure. She had little desire, she declared, to be seen in a public place conversing with such a "loose character" as himself! Indeed, she would as soon be seen talking with a common soldier — and soldiers in her day and generation were accorded scant respect since it appeared they had taken the "King's shilling" in lieu of better employment available to them. The sooner he took himself off — and his hateful little dog too — the better it would be for all concerned she flung at him. But suddenly, amused by the pained expression on his face, she had laughed merrily. Never, he assured her, had he been spoken to so disrespectfully before — and by a chit of a girl not much older than his respectful young sisters at Mossgiel. But Jean's laughter and eager capitulation had melted the ice block that had loomed between them and, tucking his bonnet beneath his arm, he had helped her gather up the spoiled linens and carry them to the pump for a fresh rinsing. "They talked and they laughed so long together," reported Nellie afterwards, that she had decided to proceed home alone. And with her went a feeling of uneasy apprehension for Jeanie, at the age of eighteen, was romantic-minded and "glaikit" (feather headed) and Robert Burns was undeniably handsome and persuasive if legend and rumour were to be believed.

No portrait exists of Jean Armour at this particular period of her life. Photography had not yet been invented and, truth to tell, there was little in the humble and mundane circumstances of her obscure life to attract the brushes and palettes of the fashionable portrait painters of the day. A little later on, however, when, as the wife of a national celebrity, she shared the spotlight focussed upon Burns, she was painted by lesser artists like Gilfillan and MacKenzie. By then, however, she was middle-aged, somewhat broad of beam and a grandmother. There is little in these later-day paintings or in the silhouettes that were executed of her during the days of her long widowhood in Dumfries, to indicate the charms that had attracted the eye of Robert Burns soon after he arrived in Mauchline. It is related by contemporary historians that her complexion was olive, her jet black eyes were clear and sparkling and her height was five foot nine, approximately that of Burns himself. She had "a bewitching smile" and an enchanting personality of the kind that can seldom be captured on canvas.

By the summer of 1785, Burns had become hopelessly in love — hopelessly because things were going badly at Mossgiel and his future looked dark — and in a poetic *Epistle* to his old friend David Sillar —who was courting a Tarbolton lass — he wrote rapturously:

> This life has joys for you and I;
> An' joys that riches ne'er could buy;
> An' joys the very best.
> There's a' the pleasures of the heart,
> The lover an' the frien';
> Ye hae your Meg, your dearest part
> An' I my darling Jean!
> It warms me, it charms me
>   To mention but her name;
> It heats, it beets me
>   An' sets me a' on flame. . . .

but by the fall of the year, James and Mary Armour, informed of their secret meetings in the shadows of the old "Castle" and on the flowery banks of the river Ayr, burned a midnight candle into the dawn, planning how they might best wean renegade young Jean away from the arms of reckless, penniless Robert Burns and into those of Robert Wilson, a respectable, plodding young weaver who had long wanted her and had now gone off to the town of Paisley to establish an independent weaver's shop that might bring him in a competence of roughly three pounds a week to enhance his matrimonial prospects in the eyes of the Armours. Before the advent of Burns in the parish, Jean had appeared willing to encourage the attentions of Wilson and to accept his escort at the Penny Reels in Hugh Morton's ballroom and at the social gatherings in the neighbouring farmhouses where the young folk gathered at the end of a hard day's work for an evening of social merriment, singing and dancing. After her first meeting with Burns, however, Jean had become increasingly reluctant to accept the advances of Wilson and sullenly declined to explain her sudden *volte face* to her hopeful parents. Robert's appealing personal magnetism, the fascination of his powerfully stimulating company and his ardent beguilements would have engulfed many a more sophisticated young woman than romantic-minded Jean. Like Lady Caroline Lamb, who wrote in her diary after meeting Lord Byron for the first time: "Mad, bad and dangerous to know; that handsome pale face is my *fate!*" Jean knew that she could never now belong to any other man.

When mason Armour declared with a resounding oath that he "would rather see the devil himself come courting his daughter" than Rab Mossgiel, he voiced a long-prevailing prejudice. His rabid hatred of Burns was no sudden phenomenon. It had matured by slow accretion over the past half a dozen years during which he had frequently visited Tarbolton on professional matters. Sometimes called upon to extend credit for the services of his apprentices, it was incumbent upon him to keep an ear well-tuned for storm-signals in the neighbourhood and tongues were loosed over the brimming bowl in the wayside taverns. He had been long familiar with reports of the financial difficulties of the Burns family at Lochlea farm and of the failing health of William Burns, head of the family, that would sooner or later place the family fortunes on the shoulders of irresponsible Robert. When, in the month of February, 1784, William Burns — worn out by the struggle to make ends meet — died peacefully in the early hours of a gray morning, an ugly little story had gone the rounds that, approaching his end, members of his family assembled at his bedside for a last paternal blessing, the tired man had declared sadly that "there was one member of the family for whose future he feared" and that Robert, turning to the window to hide his tears, had cried out brokenly: "Oh, father, is it *me* you mean?" But good William Burns, loving his passionate, headstrong first-born to the end, had turned his face to the wall, refusing to make the painful indictment.

Robert conveyed the news of his father's death to their close relative, lawyer Burness in Montrose: "I have waited to give you an account of that melancholy event which, for some time past, we have from day to day expected. Though, to be sure, we had long warning of the impending stroke, still the feelings of nature claim their part and I cannot recollect the tender endearments and parental lessons of the best of friends and ablest of instructors without feeling what, perhaps, the calmer dictates of reason would partly condemn." The words came from a deeply troubled heart for things had not been going well between Robert and his father who was dismayed by the dangerous sexual tides threatening to engulf his eldest son. Once, in a moment of paternal pride, he had remarked to his wife, Agnes Burns: "Whoever lives to see it, something extraordinary will come from that boy!" but his headstrong young colt needed a wise restraining hand on the halter and bitter words had passed increasingly between them.

It is reasonable to suppose that, long before he died, William Burns must have been fully aware that Robert was courting Lizzie Paton, his mother's raw-boned, moon-faced servant girl, in the hayloft at Lochlea after the day's work was done and that, deeply in love with Robert, the simple-hearted Lizzie was likely to deny him nothing. Agnes Burns was genuinely fond of the hard-working, agreeable girl and even urged Robert to make her his wife but Robert's brothers and sisters were horrified by the prospect claiming that poor, uneducated Lizzie with her coarse, masculine ways, would "soon sicken" Robert. Never could she be accepted as a member of the intimate family circle, at the head of Robert's table when he had a home of his own and by his side in the kirk pew, proclaiming to all the world her right to his connubial devotion.

At the breakup of the household at Lochlea and the family move to Mauchline, Lizzie had returned home to her own parish in Largieside and

Robert continued to visit her there since she was blue beneath the eyes and expecting his child.

Soon after the family settlement at Mossgiel, Agnes Burns applied to their former minister in Tarbolton for the church "transfer lines" that would entitle them all to worship in their new church and entitle them to receive a supply of the lead "tokens" that would admit them to annual Communion in the parish. Signed by the reverend Peter Wodrow, their former minister, and by his Session Clerk, the transfer lines, dated August 4th, 1784, testified to the exemplary character of the Burns family:

> There do testify that the bearers hereof, Agnes Burns, relict of the deceased William Burns, and Robert, Gilbert, Agnes and Anabella, her children, lived in the parish of Tarbolton the space of seven years and during their residence here behaved themselves soberly, honestly and free of public scandal.

Not many months were to pass, however, before "public scandal" was to resound like a clap of thunder in Mauchline for news travelled fast in rural Ayrshire and Robert's seduction of Lizzie Paton was soon out. Her child — a black-eyed female infant uncommonly like her sire — was born in the month of May and, once again, Robert's mother urged him to do the right thing by the accommodating Lizzie. He was, however, supinely non-committal in the matter. It was his first crop of wild oats. Why all the fuss and pother? Several of his own boon companions had a skeleton or two of this particular kind in their cupboards and time and the world had not stood still for them. Besides, with pressing responsibilities as head of the family now at Mossgiel, it was impossible for him to contract marriage with Lizzie Paton or any other girl. First things came first. Time enough for a halter when his feelings were more permanently engaged. Robert brazened things out and made light of his illicit paternity and he composed a defiant *jubilate* on the subject of his sins. His poem was entitled *The Poet's Welcome to his Love-begotten Daughter* and he added an explanatory note that the poem celebrated "The first instance that entitled its author to the venerable appellation of father." Tongue in cheek, he proclaimed jubilantly that the child was the "sweet fruit of many a merry dint" and rejoiced that the tiny infant was the "wee image of his bonnie Betty." He cared little for the gossip caused by the event, he declared:

> What tho' they ca' me fornicator
> An' tease my name in country clatter;
> The more they talk, I'm known the better
> E'en let them clash!
> An old wife's tongue's a feckless matter
> To gie one fash. . . .

The birth of his child — named Elizabeth after her mother — aroused in him a new and special kind of tenderness — a tenderness he was always to feel for the children he fathered. He promised to be "a loving father to her" and to see that she was as well-clad and as well-educated as "any brat in wedlock's station" and he hoped his child would inherit her mother's "person, grace and merit and her poor worthless daddy's spirit without his failings." As for the sour-faced *unco guid* and the Kirk Elders:

> As dear and near my heart I set thee
> Wi' as good will
> As a' the priests had seen me get thee
> That's out o' hell. . . .

For all his shadow-boxing, however, Robert felt his situation keenly. Informed of late by a Tarbolton friend that one of his former sweethearts had defected to a rival after he had left his old parish, he had replied that he was "glad to hear Peggy was off his hands and he was at present so taken in with a cursed affair of gallantry" that he couldn't care less about the fickle Peggy's perfidy. He promised to send Thomas Orr, his Kirkoswald correspondent, further particulars later on but Orr did not have to guess too hard as to the nature of the "cursed gallantry" poor Robert had become involved in.

Knowing that rumours of his illicit paternity were likely soon to reach the ears of his old farmer friend — Rankine of Adamhill — who had once been in a similar scrape himself, Robert composed and despatched to him a facetious *Epistle* full of the kind of Rabelaisian innuendo the bawdy-minded Rankine would doubtless enjoy:

> 'Twas ae night lately in my fun,
> I went a-rovin' wi' the gun
> An' brought a partridge to the grun'
> A bonnie hen,
> And as the twilight was begun
> Thought nane would ken.
>
> The poor wee thing was little hurt,
> I petted her a wee for sport,
> Ne'er thinking they would fash me for't
> But deil-ma-care!
> Somebody told the Poacher-court
> The whole affair.
>
> Some old used hands had ta'en a note
> That such a hen had got a shot;
> I was suspected for the plot,
> I scorned to lie
> So gat the whissle o' my groat
> An' paid the fee. . . .

As Rankine well knew, the Poacher-court was the vigilant Kirk Session and the "fee" was the usual fine imposed for parochial fornication. By means of these reluctant contributions the parish poor-boxes were maintained in a state of affluence. He was not done with his accusers yet, however, declared

the unrepentant rhymer. He intended to have full value later on for the
money that had been extracted from him:

> But, by my gun, o' guns the wale,
> An' by my powder an' my hail,
> An' by my hen an' by her tail
>   I vow and swear
> The game shall pay o'er moor and dale
>   For this next year!

> As soon as hatching time is by
> An' the wee birds begin to cry
> Lord, I'll hae sportin' by an' by
>   For my gold guinea
> Tho' I should herd the buckskin kye
>   For't in Virginia. . . .

As Rankine also knew, many a young scamp in a similar predicament had
taken off for the Americas to live down his sins while herding cattle on the
trackless ranges.

It had not taken Robert long to discover that, in the business of sniffing
out parochial sin, Mauchline Kirk Session was every bit as competent as the
Session had been in his old parish. A triumvirate of sour-faced Elders —
among them an elderly bachelor named William Fisher who was accused of
questioning the girls too intimately on matters likely to bring them to the
cutty stool — paraded up and down the highways and byways on the Sabbath
day, peering through uncurtained windows and into open doorways to
apprehend those absent from church services — their cash contributions
lost to the collection plates. Upon William Fisher's despicable head, Robert
unleashed all the scorn he felt for such hypocrites. His poem *Holy Willie's
Prayer* soon had the local taverns in a roar:

> O Lord! Thou kens what zeal I bear
> When drinkers drink an' swearers swear,
> An' singin' there and dancin' here
>   Wi' great an' sma';
> For I am keepit by Thy fear
>   Free from them a'.

> But yet, O Lord! confess I must
> At times I'm fash'd wi' fleshly lust
>   Vile self gets in:
> But Thou remembers we are dust
>   Defil'd in sin.

> O Lord! yestre'en, Thou kens, wi' Meg —
> Thy pardon I sincerely beg;
> O! may it ne'er be livin' plague
>   To my dishonour
> An' I'll never lift a lawless leg
>   Again upon her.

Besides, I further must allow
Wi' Lizzie's lass three times I trow;
But, Lord, that Friday I was fu'
    When I came near her
Or else Thou kens Thy servant true
    Would ne'er have steer'd her. . . .

In fourteen sparkling, lethal stanzas Poet Burns made mincemeat of Holy Willie's pious pretences and, encouraged by his success, sharpened his quill for assault upon other parochial cankers. Fierce contention raged between two conflicting religous factions in the community — the "Auld Lights" and the "New Lights." The former clung to the timeworn tenets of fire and brimstone for unrepentant sinners; the latter sought to break free from a religious tyranny that stemmed from the days of Calvin and his disciples and took a more benign view of the sins of parishioners. The discord was tailor-made for Robert's thrusting pen and in no time at all a new batch of poems circulated in the taverns and in the kitchens of wayside farmhouses. These included *The Twa Herds or the Holy Quarrel; The Ordination; The Holy Fair* and an *Address to the Unco Guid or Rigidly Righteous.* He also composed a whimsical *Address to the Deil* in which he begged for tolerance for sinners like himself:

Hear me, Auld Hangie, for a wee
An' let poor damnéd bodies be;
I'm sure sma' pleasure it can gie
    E'en to a Deil
To skelp an' scold poor dogs like me
    An' hear us squeal. . . .

Wishing to ingratiate himself with his new landlord, Gavin Hamilton — who had been hailed before the Session on certain trumpery charges — he composed a lively defence. Hamilton, a highly respected man, had been accused of "unnecessary absence from church on five successive Sundays; setting out on a journey to Carrick on the Sabbath day; habitual, if not total neglect of family worship; and writing an abusive letter to the Session." He had also been accused of allowing a servant to dig potatoes on the Sabbath day — not only to dig them but to take them into the house. The rows of potatoes had been carefully measured to point up his guilt. Each row measured eleven and a half feet, making a sum total of twenty feet of illicitly harvested tubers. Furious with his mealy-mouthed accusers who appeared to have run out of sin-sniffing objectives, Hamilton took his case to a higher ecclesiastical court in Ayr and won speedy acquittal. In a *Dedication to Gavin Hamilton* Robert lashed out at his accusers and their "three-mile prayers and half-mile graces":

Their sighin', cantin', grace-proud faces
    Their stretchin' conscience,
Whose greed, revenge and pride disgraces
    Worse than their nonsense. . . .

They "took religion in their mouth and gave their malice scope on some poor wight, hunting him down to ruin," he declared. He detested their "hollow hearts" and the "hocus-pocus" they dispensed "to cheat the crowd." As for himself, he opined:

> God knows I'm not the thing I should be
> Nor am I even the thing I could be
> But twenty times I sooner would be
>   An atheist clean
> Than under gospel colours hid be
>   Just for a screen.
>
> An honest man may like a glass,
> An honest man may like a lass,
> But mean revenge an' malice false
>   He'll still disdain
> An' then cry zeal for gospel laws
>   Like some we ken. . . .

He was already in exceedingly bad odour with the Session for his part in Lizzie Paton's undoing and he had been publicly rebuked for his fornication in Mauchline Parish Church (Lizzie received her rebuke in her own parish) but poetic assaults like these, drifting inevitably into the hands of "God's Elect", did little to recommend him to the goodwill of the Session. With two of his boon companions — both of whom were notorious for their amorous misdemeanors — he had organized a mock *Court of Equity* for the trial of village fornicators who refused to acknowledge their responsibilities towards the girls they had seduced and were punished by ducking at the village pump. Robert's audacious poem eventually found its way into the hands of a shocked James Armour and, once again, he forbade him the house and the company of his daughters.

CHAPTER 3

In spite of pressing anxieties at Mossgiel in these early days when every member of the family was bending a shoulder to the wheel — Agnes Burns and the girls working harder than ever in the dairy to produce the sweet milk cheese for which they were earning a good reputation; the menfolk in the fields, the barn and the byre — Robert managed to find time to attend the local Fairs and to look the girls over thoroughly. His findings showed up in a new poem entitled *The Mauchline Belles* similar to one entitled *The Tarbolton Lasses* he had written in his old parish:

> In Mauchline there dwells six proper young belles,
> The pride o' the place an' its neighbourhood a',
> Their carriage and dress a stranger would guess
> In London or Paris they'd gotten it a'.
>
> Miss Miller is fine, Miss Markland's divine,
> Miss Smith she has wit and Miss Betty is braw,
> There's beauty an' fortune to get wi' Miss Morton,
> But Armour's the jewel for me o' them a'.

And, knowing that the Paton scandal was a conversation piece in the village — for baby Bess had been brought to Mossgiel for rearing — he also composed a song warning the girls that a black sheep had come among them and had better be avoided:

> O, leave novels, ye Mauchline belles,
> Ye're safer at your spinning-wheel;
> Such witching books are baited hooks
> For rakish rooks like Rob Mossgiel.
>
> Your fine "Tom Jones" and "Grandisons"
> They make your youthful fancies reel;
> They heat your brains and fire your veins
> An' then ye're prey for Rob Mossgiel.

Beware a tongue that's smoothly hung,
A heart that warmly seems to feel;
That feeling heart but acts a part
'Tis rakish art in Rob Mossgiel.

The frank address, the soft caress
Are worse than polished darts of steel;
The frank address and *politesse*
Are all *finesse* in Rob Mossgiel.

Soon after settling at Mossgiel he had received, as head of the family, a parcel of tax forms from the Tax Collector in Ayr on which to declare his assets for the benefit of William Pitt who, from a stately perch in London, was combing the length and breadth of Scotland — an unwilling milch cow — for taxes to liquidate a staggering national debt. Taxable assets, it appeared, included "farm equipment, hired help, farm beasts and wheeled conveyances" and Robert set to work to compose a poetic mock "Inventory" for the amusement of his old friend Tax Collector Aiken in Ayr. His assets were negligible, he reported. "Heaven had sent him one more than he wanted" in the person of "sonsie, smirkin' dear-bought Bess." He "refused to pay a tax on either her or her mother." He had "paid enough for them already." He would promise, however, to mend his unregenerate ways in the future:

Frae this time forth, I do declare
I'll ne'er ride horse nor hussy more;
Thro' dirt and dub for life I'll paddle
Ere I so dear pay for a saddle . . .
The Kirk an' you can tak' you that!
It puts but little in your pat!

Carriage horses? None — though he did have "four plough-horses of gallant mettle." One of them was "a good old has-been that had been strong and willing all its days." Another was a "well-going filly that had often brought him safely home from Kilmarnock after a carousal at the inn." The rear horse on the plough was "as worthy a beast as ever wore hide or rope" but the fourth animal was "a stubborn, capricious, stark mad beast that had been named Highland Donald for its sins." In addition he owned a promising young colt — "the best that ever ran before a tail." It should fetch fifteen pounds if it lived to maturity. "Conveyances?" That story, too, was soon told. He owned "three carts, one of them almost new" and if the Tax Collector should be interested in wheelbarrows, he had one with a broken leg and broken handles. He had made a poker out of its spindle and his mother had burned its wheel. Next, there was the matter of "Farm Servants." He employed three young lads notable for noisy behaviour and exceedingly healthy appetites. One of them assisted him when ploughing — running in front of the plough to clear away small obstacles with the pettle in order that the shears might not be damaged; the second lad assisted with the threshing in the barn while "Wee Davock" — the youngest and smartest of them all and "not much higher than his employer's leg" — helped with the feeding of the beasts. All of them were examined each day in the Catechism — an employer's responsibility to the Kirk Session. As to "Female Servants" — he had none: "Lord keep me free o' a' temptation!" Neither did he have a wife — "an' that my bliss is, an' ye hae laid no tax on Misses!" He added his signature to the rhymed "Inventory" and dated it February 22, 1784.

The small farmhouse of Mossgiel, previously renovated for occupancy by Gavin Hamilton, was filled by the Burns family to capacity. It boasted two small rooms — a "but and ben" or parlour and kitchen on the ground floor and above, with access by ladder from a lobby behind the front door, were three small rooms that served as sleeping quarters and storage accommodation. The middle of the three rooms was shared by Robert and Gilbert and under its tiny skylight window, nestled deep in the thatch, Robert placed his desk — a small deal table with a single drawer in which he kept his papers, letters, songs and poems and his Commonplace Book. On the desk was a battered horn candle-holder, an assortment of goose-quills and a dish of sand for blotting purposes.

During the spring and summer of 1785, when his passion for Jean Armour ran high, his pen was constantly employed and notwithstanding discouraging weather conditions, a fatal investment in poor seed and mounting family expenses during the failure of crops, Robert composed most of the poems that were later to make him famous — *Halloween, The Jolly Beggars, The Cotter's Saturday Night, The Holy Fair, Rantin' Rovin' Robin, The Twa Dogs, Address to the Deil, The Auld Farmer's New Year Salute to his Auld Mare Maggie, Death and Doctor Hornbook* and, following in quick succession, *The Vision, Address to the Unco Guid, To a Louse, To a Mountain Daisy, The Lass o' Ballochmyle, Nature's Law, A Winter's Night, Address to the Toothache, The Brigs o' Ayr, Tam Samson's Elegy, To a Mouse* and numerous *Epistles* and *Epigrams*. His rhymed *Epistles* were the delight of his friends and his clever *Epigrams* — not always in the best of taste and often downright offensive — were read with relish in the thronged taverns where Jean sometimes joined Rab for a convivial hour.

His epic poem, *The Holy Fair* was a rousing success amongst his eager cronies. It was a shrewd and derisive burlesque of the annual Communion services that were held in the parish kirkyard and gave Robert immense scope for his special talents as a satirical observer. It was a bold man, indeed, who dared to unleash contempt for observances that were sacrosanct to the Kirk Session and faithful communicants and even those who heard the poem read secretly, at first, were aghast at its author's effrontery. To participate in the day-long Communion services came half a dozen clerics from afar to assist the reverend William Auld, the local minister, in the business of sin-purging and salvation of souls. Working in relays from sun-up to sun-down, the visiting Divines mounted a rostrum or "tent" to wrestle with the Devil for the souls of the unregenerate and, wearying occasionally of the long spates of fiery oratory and pulpit-thumping, members of the congregation drifted into the nearby taverns for a refreshing tankard of ale and a bite of the fresh-baked bread and cheese they had brought along with them to allay the pangs of hunger. To Robert, with a keen sense of the ridiculous, the proceedings were convulsing. Here was "Black Russell" — a sour-faced cleric from Kilmarnock — droning on and on about the devouring flames of hell, his hearers — many of whom had fallen asleep — awakening suddenly with a start, believing they were hearing the crackle of the consuming flames — only to find "it was a neighbour snorin'." And here was "Wee Miller" — a pint-sized minister from Kilmaurs — who privately doubted some of the dogma he was called upon to dispense but had to walk warily because he needed a new manse. And here were the officious "Black Bonnets" who passed the collection plates endlessly and glowered disapprovingly at the poor widow's mite.

Delighted as she was with Robert's most recent poem and with the thunderous applause that had greeted it when he read it aloud in Nanse Tinnock's inn, Jean could only hope fervently that *The Holy Fair* would not come to the ears of her parents who were pillars of the Church. From time to time, when her father was away from home on one of his professional jaunts and her mother was visiting neighbours or relatives or was busy with the younger bairns, she often signalled to Robert, waiting in the Whitefoord Arms nearby, from an upstairs window of her home in the Cowgate and sometimes managed to slip across the intervening courtyard to join him there:

> Where Burns cam' weary frae the plough
> To hae a crack wi' Johnnie Dow
> On nights at e'en
> An' whiles to taste the mountain dew
> Wi Bonnie Jean. . . .

She knew all about the Paton affair and the financial difficulties at Mossgiel. She knew about Gavin Hamilton's unpaid rent — a frequent topic at the Armour breakfast table — and she had heard disturbing rumours that Robert was secretly meeting Mary Campbell, the Hamilton's young nursemaid, in the shadows of the old "Castle" when she was unable to meet him. And she was long familiar with local gossip that "Mossgiel" was spending far too much time with idle companions in the taverns and too much money that should have gone to liquidate debts to Gavin Hamilton; but, wrapped protectively in Robert's rough woollen plaid, fragrant with peat smoke, his cheek tenderly brushing hers, his lips gentle and sweet, she only knew that she loved him desperately and could deny him nothing.

Robert Wilson was now many miles away and was counting less and less with her as the days of his absence wore on. Resolutely, at first — perhaps because the Paton affair had been a sobering lesson — she had resisted Robert's ardours but by the end of the year she had given herself to him and, early in the spring of 1786, she had been obliged to confess to her mother that she was pregnant.

The news fell like a thunderbolt on the ears of her father, the mason, who, receiving the staggering tidings after a particularly hard day's riding, fainted from shock while Mary Armour rushed for a cordial to revive him. No need to ask, thundered the mason, who was the scoundrel who had fouled his nest. A thousands curses on profligate Burns — so much older than Jean — who could not even put a roof over her head in the hour of her extremity and was not likely to do so. Far into the night, until the pale dawn light filtered through the windows of the Armour cottage in the Cowgate, mason Armour roared and stormed and vowed vengeance upon the head of his daughter's despoiler.

Summoned before him the following day, white and trembling in every nerve, Jean proffered a "paper" Robert had given her that proclaimed her his lawful wife. The Church, which only accepted the ecclesiastical form of marriage, might not accept the provisions of "Irregular Marriage" but the laws of Scotland did, Robert had assured her and, knowing that he had many competent legal friends to advise him — among them Gavin Hamilton of Mauchline and Robert Aiken of Ayr and several young friends who were law apprentices in Edinburgh — she had readily accepted his representations.

Snatching the "paper" from her trembling hand, James Armour had spat in the peat fire on the hearth and called her a terrible name. His face purple and ashen in turn, his eyes blazing with rage, he had staggered from the parlour like a man struck with fork-lightning, flinging Jean from him with an ugly oath as, on her knees before him, she had begged pitifully for forgiveness and comfort — if not for her own sake, for the sake of the little child to be. Her anguished pleas fell on deaf ears, however, and the slamming of the door behind her father as he left the room, sounded like a deathknell in her ears. Creeping upstairs to the bedroom she shared with her younger sister Nellie, she had sobbed all night until a pale dawn light broke over the cobblestones of the Cowgate and she heard the brisk clip-clop of the hooves of her father's pony as he set out for the town of Ayr to consult his lawyer there. Never would he accept Robert Burns as a son-in-law, he had sworn to his wife, adding malevolently that, had the law allowed it, he would have been glad to break a stick over the shoulders of the scamp at Mossgiel. By hook or by crook, by fair means or foul, the "marriage paper" must be destroyed beyond all hope of resuscitation. Child or no child, he would never accept Robert Burns as a member of his intimate family circle.

Returning from Ayr the following day, mason Armour cleared the decks for parental action. The "marriage paper" had met the fate it deserved at the hands of lawyer Aiken, he told Jean. It had been destroyed by the simple expedient of cutting out the names of the contracting parties. "Marriage paper," indeed, he had ranted, ramming a huge pinch of snuff up his quivering nostrils. Everybody but Jean, it seemed, knew what happened to unfortunate young women who relied upon such piecrust promises! If *both* parties adhered to the covenant of "Irregular Marriage" all might be well but the circuit courts bulged with petitions for dissolution by one or other of the parties who had grown tired of their bargain and wanted to be free. Sometimes these petitions were granted — usually when no offspring were involved — but sometimes they were not. It all depended, it appeared, on the whim, mood or digestion of the presiding Justices. Besides, there were realistic questions to be asked and answered. What provision was Burns able to make for a wife and child when he could not even pay the Mossgiel rent? What about the failure of the crops likely to pyramid his indebtedness to his landlord? What about the prior claim of his child by Lizzie Paton should she decide to sue for infant maintenance? And what about the persisting rumours that Burns was conducting a clandestine courtship of Mary Campbell under their very nose? Was it not possible, indeed, that Mary Campbell might, at this very time, be pregnant herself? And how was Jean to fare under these bleak possibilities?

Not only had Robert fallen out with the Kirk Session, but he was aiming his shafts at respectable citizens who had never done him any harm and his popularity was waning in circles that might have been tolerant of his misdoings. He had composed — and publicly read — certain offensive *Epitaphs* and *Epigrams,* among them one which degraded a local mason named Humphrey:

> Below these stones lie Jamie's bones;
> O' Death! it's my opinion
> Thou ne'er took such a bleth'rin' bitch
> Into thy dark dominions.

He had also composed an *Epigram on a Henpecked Country Squire* whose wife, residing in a mansion called Netherplace, close by, was secretly accused of penuriousness; and he had written some defamatory lines about the Earl of Galloway who, somehow or other, had incurred his dislike:

> What dost thou in that mansion fair?
> Flit, Galloway, and find
> Some narrow, dirty dungeon cave
> The picture of thy mind.
>
> No Stewart art thou, Galloway,
> The Stewarts all were brave;
> Besides, the Stewarts all were fools,
> Not one of them a *knave.*

> Bright ran thy line, O Galloway!
> Through many a fair-famed sire;
> So ran the far-famed Roman Way —
> So ended — in a mire!

Such gratuitous insults, aimed at high and low alike, were in execrable taste and it was only a matter of time, some thought, when Burns of Mossgiel would be booted out of the parish by those who cowered under his effrontery and had money to expedite his exit.

The Armours decided that Jean must be packed off to her aunt Purdie in Paisley since the vigilant Kirk Elders would soon come knocking on the door to investigate the truth of the current rumours. Effectively separated from Burns and from his corroding influence, she might be able to induce the faithful Wilson there to renew his suit and to shoulder her child as his own. Utterly dependent now on the goodwill of her parents, Jean tearfully packed her box and sent word to Robert at Mossgiel that he must make no attempt to see her again. Nor should he send any messages to the Cowgate or attempt to visit her there.

News of her supine capitulation to the summary demands of her parents enraged Robert. Not only was he to be deprived of her stimulating company but, in due course, he was likely to be denied access to his own flesh and blood — the child she was to bear. Disregarding her warning that he must not show his face in the Cowgate again, he rode over to Mauchline and, in a painful interview with mason Armour, offered to turn over his interest in the farm to his brother and to seek immediate employment as a common labourer to support Jean and her child. Alternatively, he suggested he might seek profitable employment for a time in the West Indies until such time as he was able to assume the full responsibilities of marriage. To all these persuasions, however, mason Armour turned a deliberately deaf ear and indicated that he would countenance no further visits. Defeated and anguished, Robert rode back to Mossgiel and, during the painful days that followed, poured out his misery in a series of poignant poems — *The Lament; To Ruin;* and *Despondency an Ode*. Repudiation by Jean herself had been hardest to bear — and on this point mason Armour had left him no possible doubt. Her vows of fidelity, come what might, had seemed so inviolable:

> O! can she bear so base a heart,
>   So lost to honour, lost to truth,
> As from the fondest lover part,
>   The plighted husband of her youth!
> Alas! life's path may be unsmooth;
>   Her way may lie thro' rough distress;
> Then who her pangs and pains will soothe,
>   Her sorrows share and make them less.
>
> Encircled in her clasping arms
>   How have the raptur'd moments flown!

> How have I wished for fortune's charms
> For her dear sake and hers alone!
> And must I think it! Is she gone —
> My secret heart's exulting boast?
> And does she heedless hear my groan?
> And is she ever, ever lost?

In a state bordering on hysteria, he deplored to a friend "a faithless woman's broken vow" and indicated a determination to go abroad in an attempt to forget that "a jillet had broken his heart." He tried in vain to banish the visual image of Jean from his mind but he was crucified by recollection of the golden hours they had shared together. Ploughing his fields at Mossgiel one day and in a deeply retrospective mood, he had razed a tiny field daisy — one of many he had razed, unheeded, before — and in its fate he saw a parallel to the fate of Jean who was now three months pregnant:

> Wee, modest, crimson-tippéd flow'r
> Thou's met me in an evil hour;
> But I maun crush among the stoure
> Thy tender stem;
> To spare thee now is past my pow'r
> Thou bonnie gem!

Jean's youth and inexperience, her trusting faith, tormented him and his pen was heavy with grief and self-condemnation:

> Cold blew the bitter-biting north
> Upon thy early humble birth,
> Yet cheerfully thou glinted forth
> Amid the storm,
> Scarce rear'd above the parent earth
> Thy tender form.
>
> There in thy scanty mantle clad,
> Thy snowy bosom sunwards spread,
> Thou lifts thy unassuming head
> In humble guise
> But now the plough upturns thy bed
> And low thou lies.
>
> Such is the fate of artless maid,
> Sweet flow'ret of the rural shade,
> By love's simplicity betray'd
> And guileless trust,
> Till she, like thee, all soil'd is laid
> Low in the dust. . . .

He sent a copy of the poem to his friend John Kennedy who was factor at Dumfries House, adding a note that would enable Kennedy to read between the lines: "I am a good deal pleased with the sentiments this poem expresses as they are the feelings of a heart melancholy has marked for its own."

Not long before, when his love for Jean had been at its starry meridian and his material prospects at their lowest, he had composed an introspective poem reflecting his unfortunate state. Turning up the nest of a tiny field mouse while ploughing one day, he had seen in its plight a reflection of his own:

> That wee bit heap o' leaves an' stibble
> Has cost thee mony a weary nibble!
> Now thou's turned out, for a' thy trouble
>   Nor house nor hold
> To bear the winter's sleety dribble
>   An' hoar-frost cold!
>
> But, Mousie, thou art no thy lane
> In proving foresight may be vain:
> The best-laid schemes o' mice an' men
>   Gang aft agley,
> An' leave us nought but grief an' pain
>   For promised joy.
>
> Still, thou art blest compar'd wi' me!
> The present only toucheth thee:
> But, och! I backward cast my e'e
>   On prospects drear;
> An' forward tho' I canna see
>   I guess and fear.

Assailed by poverty, as his father had been before him, and beset with disasters at Mossgiel, the rosy dreams he had cherished of a happy future with Jean by his side had vanished like the mists off the face of Ben Lomond. Poverty was the greatest of all scourges, he believed. Making a token payment to a friend to whom he was in debt a few years later he gave rein to a bitter denunciation of the poverty that had always dogged him: "Take these two guineas and place them over and above that damned account of yours which has gagged my mouth these five or six months," he wrote Peter Hill, Edinburgh bookseller. "O, the supreme curse of making three guineas do the business of five! Not all the labours of Hercules nor all the Hebrews' three centuries of Egyptian bondage were such an insuperable business, such an infernal task! Poverty! thou half-sister of Death, thou cousin-german of Hell!" and to his self-confessed sins of pride and passion he added a bitter and unreasoning hatred of those whose purses were well-lined and whose stomachs were comfortably full. It was a prejudice that had once been pinpointed by his brother Gilbert who told an early biographer that "when young, Robert always had a particular jealousy of people who were richer than himself or had more consequence in life" and that when he selected the girls he wished to court he "rarely settled on persons of this description." His personal bias against those who were comfortably heeled was to be mirrored in many of his adult poems and in his letters to intimate friends.

It reached its apogee in the song he composed for Thomson's *Collection* on New Year's Day in 1795 entitled *For a' That, and a' That,* the first stanza of which proclaimed:

> Is there for honest Poverty
> That hangs his head, and a' that?
> The coward-slave, we pass him by,
> We dare be poor, for a' that!
> For a' that, and a' that,
> Our toils obscure, and a' that,
> The rank is but the guinea's stamp,
> The man's the gold for a' that.

He was convinced that, but for his own condition of chronic poverty, mason Armour might have been willing to condone his shortcomings but he was unwilling to concede that James Armour was merely conforming to the pattern of parental responsibility towards a young attractive and somewhat flighty young daughter. Time was to bring Burns a daughter of his own and to wring from him a confession that he felt "unequal to rearing girls" and preferred male children. "Besides," he told Frances Dunlop, "girls should always have money!" If Jean had not been so totally dependent upon her heartless parents and if he himself had only been able to provide her with a "downsetting," how different things might have been for them both!

CHAPTER 4

Seldom venturing into the village now since he had little desire to encounter any of the hateful Armour clan or to suffer the sour looks and averted heads of Mauchline's *unco guid,* Robert had little way of knowing how Jean fared or how soon she was likely to return from Paisley to face interrogation at the hands of the prying Kirk Session. Like many another unfortunate young woman in her situation, she would be questioned first privately in the vestry and she would be ordered to appear publicily on the cutty stool on three successive Sundays for ecclesiastical rebuke. It was a shattering ordeal that had caused many a girl to take her own life and that of her unborn child rather than face her smirking accusers. The proceedings were traditional — the congregation assembled as if for a Roman holiday; the white-faced trembling culprits lined up side by side, male and female, in full view of all.

Mounting the rostrum and clearing his throat ominously, the reverend William Auld would peer over the rim of his horn spectacles at the accused and deliver the long-familiar denunciation that was written down in his well-thumbed little black book:

> You appear there to be rebuked and, at the same time, making a profession repentance for the sin of fornication. The frequency of this sin is just matter of lamentation among Christians and affords just ground of deep humiliation to the guilty persons themselves. . . .

and here the reverend William Auld would pause significantly while the blushing penitents braced themselves for his final blast:

> We call upon you to reflect seriously in contrition of heart, on all the instances of your guilt; on their numbers, high aggravation and unhappy consequences; and say — having done grievously — we'll do so no more. *Beware of returning to your sin* as some of you have done like the dog to his vomit or the sow that was washed to her wallowing in the mire.

The crisp shutting of his little black book would sound like the crack of doom in the awful silence. There would be a rustling of hymnbooks, a tide of whispering and ill-concealed sniggers and a scratching of pens in the vestry where the proceedings were entered in the Kirk Session minute book. The Elders of the church prided themselves on their creditable record in the matter of bringing parish sinners to the Stool. "Notwithstanding the great noise in the parish, there were only twenty fornicators since last Sacrament," they had recorded proudly. In the parish of Dundonald, not very far away, the Session had recorded considerable head-scratching when John Hay of Paulstone "confessed fornication with Janet Sillar and Mary Campbell; also with Euphan Bowie from the New Town of Ayr and was the father of a child by each of them." He had also confessed fornication with Margaret Courdie and Agnes McCletchie and had been ordered to "confess publicly any day he pleased" — any day that might be spared from his sexual foraging.

Jean returned to Mauchline early in June to find a summons from the Kirk Session to appear before them for preliminary interrogation and, shrinking from the ordeal of subjecting herself to a painful humiliation, she signed a confession prepared for her signature by her father:

> I am heartily sorry that I have given and must give your Session trouble on my account. I acknowledge that I am with child and that Robert Burns in Mossgiel is the father. I am, with great respect, your most humble servant
>
> Jean Armour.

"Humble servant" and "great respect", these were the tributes that were rendered up to the tyrannous Kirk Session by every trembling girl who had done what came naturally for love of a lad. "A Scotch girl stands in terrible awe of the Scottish Kirk," wrote the poet Keats who once visited Ayrshire, "Poor little Susannas, they will scarcely laugh — they are greatly to be pitied and the Kirk is greatly to be damned. These Kirkmen have done Scotland harm — they have banished puns and laughing and kissing. They have made men, women, old men, young men, young women, girls and infants *careful*. I would rather be a wild hog than be the occasion of a Poor Creature's pennance before these execrable Elders," and he related that, during a visit to Dumfries and the Mausoleum of Burns he had met an engaging young chambermaid who was "fair, kind and ready to laugh because she was out of the domination of the Scotch Kirk."

During Jean's absence in Paisley rumours had drifted into Mauchline that Robert Wilson, her former lover, had been visiting her frequently at her aunt's home and had "given her money to relieve her necessities," and that the faithful Wilson had promised to marry nobody else as long as she remained free. The rumours crucified Robert. Did he not know how warm and generous — how willing — Jean was in certain directions and how anxious she would be to find some solution to her difficulties? The thought

30

of her in the arms of Wilson tormented him day and night and nagged at him constantly. Sometimes, by the fireside at Mossgiel, after the day's work was done, he visualized her preparing forlornly for her coming ordeal and his conscience troubled him. Once he had composed for Lizzie Paton, in similar circumstances, a poem that, with a little polishing, might serve to mirror Jean's own feelings at the moment:

> O, who my babie clothes will buy?
> O' who will tend me when I cry?
> Who will kiss me where I lie?
>> The rantin' dog the daddie o't.
>
> O, who will own he did the fault?
> O, who will buy my groanin' malt?
> O, who will tell me how to ca't?
>> The rantin' dog the daddie o't.
>
> When I mount the creepie chair,
> Who will sit beside me there?
> Give me Rab, I'll seek nae mair —
>> The rantin' dog the daddie o't.
>
> Who will chat to me when lane?
> Who will make me fond again?
> Who will kiss me o'er again?
> The rantin' dog the daddie o't.

In conspiring with his lawyer in Ayr to destroy the "paper" Burns had given his daughter to cover her emergency, James Armour had been motivated by two feelings — deep-rooted, long-standing dislike of Burns (based on his past record in Tarbolton and on his behaviour since coming to Mauchline) and a desire to free Jean from what he believed would be a disastrous union. Which of these motivations predominated it is difficult to assess at this late day but, in any event, it would seem that the mason and his consultant were on legally unsound ground when they chose to believe that the cutting out of the signatures or names recorded in the "paper" automatically voided the union. Chambers, an early biographer of Burns, submitted the matter to a competent legal authority whose considered verdict was as follows:

BURNS'S MARRIAGE: WAS IT EVER ANNULLED?

A marriage once existing cannot be annulled but by a divorce. The destruction of the document may place impediments in the way of proving a marriage may have existed — just as the burning of a bloody shirt may render it more difficult to prove a murder; but the *fact* cannot be altered.

The question is, then: Was there a marriage between Burns and Jean Armour? Certainly there was if the document destroyed was a declaration by Burns that Jean Armour was his wife, or that he had married her and she accepted it in that light at the time. The following from *Erskine* will show that the rule is much older than Burns's day:

"Marriage may without doubt be perfected by the consent of the parties declared in writing, provided the writing be so conceived as necessary to impart their present consent. The proof of marriage is not confined to the testimony of the clergyman and witnesses present at a ceremony. The subsequent acknowledgment of it by the parties concerned is sufficient to support the marriage if it appear to have been made, not in a jocular manner, but seriously and with deliberation."

Undoubtedly, if Burns had married anyone else, he would have been guilty of bigamy.

There is a shrewd suspicion in the minds of Armour descendants today, however, that James Armour, in his desire to free his daughter from what he considered a calamitous union, had somehow or other been able to persuade lawyer Aiken of Ayr — who must have been fully conversant with the laws of the country as they pertained to "irregular marriage" — to enter into a ploy that removal of the names in the paper automatically voided the union. Moreover, it is possible that mason Armour, knowing that his daughter knew little or nothing of such affairs, might have hazarded a guess that unhappy Jean — all too familiar with rumours of Robert's attentions to Mary Campbell — might be willing to believe that he had deceived her as to the honourable intentions inherent in the document he had given her. As Aiken must have known and must surely have pointed out to James Armour, three different forms of "irregular marriage" were valid in Scotland at that time under the provisions of the Irregular Marriage Act which had been chiefly promulgated to protect the rights of resulting children. A man and woman might live together openly "by habit and repute." Alternatively, a couple might simply declare themselves man and wife and no witness was necessary although if, at a later date, a petition was instituted for dissolution of the ties, the testimony of a witness might be valuable. The third form of "marriage" allowable under the Act permitted a couple to promise registered marriage at some future date — often when their financial status had become more stable — and if, after such mutual promise, and in reliance upon it, the female allowed intimacy or conjugal rights, that fact, of itself, established a marriage. The essence of marriage was *consent* and the establishment of a mutual continuing relationship implied consent though the law governing such regulations was not then as crystal clear as it was later to become.

Deeply shocked and wounded by what he considered Jean's perfidy in consenting to abandon him and, because his pride was so hurt he had little stomach to pursue the legalities of their situation, Robert now decided to petition the Kirk Session for a certificate indicating his bachelor status and to go abroad with the certificate in his pocket. He had little doubt but that the Church — which only recognized ecclesiatical marriage—would readily comply. It based its authority in such matters upon the edict of its General

Assembly of 1571 proclaiming that "because the conjunction of marriage pertaineth to the Ministry, the causes of adherence and divorcement also pertain to them as naturally annexed thereto." Once he had done pennance in the Church for fornication with Jean, the Kirk Session would have little justification for regarding him as a married man since no ecclesiastical marriage had followed thanks to the faithless Jean and her scheming father.

Robert's private letters to intimate friends at this juncture were revealing. In a letter to his Ayrshire farmer friend Ballantine he reported:

> Old Armour prevailed with him (Aiken) to mutilate that unlucky paper yesterday. Would you believe it? Though I had not a hope nor even a wish to make her mine after her conduct, yet when he told me the names were all out of the paper, my heart died within me and he cut my veins with the news

and he wrote to David Brice, his shoemaker friend now in Glasgow, relating:

> Poor, ill-advised Armour came home from Paisley on Friday last. You have heard all the particulars of that affair, and a black affair it is. What she thinks of her conduct now, I don't know; one thing I do know — she has made me completely miserable. Never man loved, or rather adored, a woman more than I did her, and, to confess a truth between you and me, I do still love her to distraction after all, though I won't tell her so if I were to see her, which I don't want to do . . . I can have no nearer idea of the place of eternal punishment that what I have felt in my own breast on her account. I have tried often to forget her; I have run into all kinds of dissipation and riots, mason-meetings, drinking matches and other mischief to drive her out of my head, but all in vain

and he let Brice into the secret of his intended emigration to the West Indies:

> And now for a grand cure: the ship is on her way home that is to take me out to Jamaica; and then, farewell dear old Scotland! and farewell dear ungrateful Jean! for never, never will I see you more. . . .

To John Richmond, once clerk to Gavin Hamilton in Mauchline but now apprenticed to a lawyer in Edinburgh, he confided his plans for acquiring a bachelor's certificate from the Kirk Session in Mauchline before departing abroad:

> I have visited Armour since her return home; not from the least view of reconciliation, but merely to ask after her health and, to you I will confess it, from a foolish hankering fondness, very ill-placed indeed. The mother forbade me the house, nor did Jean show the penitence that might have been expected. However, the minister, I am informed, will give me a certificate as a single man if I comply with the rules of the church, which, for that very reason, I intend to do.

A fortnight later he penned another line to Brice, bringing him up to date on most recent developments:

I have already appeared publicly in church and was indulged in the liberty of standing in my own seat. I did this to get a certificate as a bachelor which Mr. Auld promised me. Jean and her friends (relatives) insisted that she should stand along with me in the kirk but the minister would not allow it which bred a great trouble, I assure you, and I am blamed as the cause of it all, though I am sure I am innocent; but I am very much pleased for all that not to have had her company. I am now fixed to go to the West Indies in October.

His reference to "standing alone in his own seat" instead of side by side with Jean in the common line-up of fornicators was somewhat ambiguous but it might appear that, in view of his petition for a bachelor's certificate as a single man, the Kirk Session, guided by the reverend William Auld who had promised the boon, may have considered that a solo appearance in his own seat was advisable. It was a privilege sometimes extended to the more important penitents but it would be a bitter pill for the Armours to swallow to see their daughter, unpaired in the kirk, standing alone like a common prostitute, among the parish sinners. It would humble their pride and delight their enemies, Robert rejoiced, though his heart was torn by his own disloyalty to Jean in a distressing hour.

But James Armour was not yet done with the machinations of the fly-by-night Burns whose box, it was reported, was already packed for his flight, and he instructed his lawyer to issue a writ in *meditatione fugare* to compel him to support the coming child. "Would you believe it?", Robert wrote Richmond again, "Armour has got a warrant to throw me in jail till I find security for an enormous sum. This they keep an entire secret but I got it by a channel they little dream of. I am wandering from one friend's house to another (to escape service of the writ) and, like a true son of the Gospel, have nowhere to lay my head. I know you will pour an execration on her head, but spare the poor, ill-advised girl, for my sake; though may all the Furies that rend the injur'd, enrag'd Lover's bosom await the old Harridan, her mother, until her latest hour!" and he concluded with a vindictive curse: "May Hell string the arm of Death to throw the fatal dart and all the winds of warring elements rouse the infernal flames to welcome her approach! For Heaven's sake, burn this letter and never show it to a living creature. I write in a moment of rage, reflecting on my miserable situation — exiled, abandoned, forlorn. I can write no more . . . "

It was the smug-faced Mary Armour he hated most of all. It was she who had slammed the door in his face on his last visit to the Cowgate and she who had denounced him to all and sundry in the village. Left alone for a time to cool his wrath, mason Armour might perhaps be counted upon to take a more realistic man-to-man view of events but in the two-headed she-dragon, Mary Armour, he had a relentless foe.

His bachelor's certificate soon in his pocket, he speeded up his plans for going abroad since he was anxious to shake the dust of Mauchline from his feet forever. Through the influence of an Ayrshire friend who had a relative in Jamaica, he obtained a position there with a Dr. Douglas. Employment was to be for a three-year period and the salary offered was £30 per annum. He did not know where he would be able to lay his hands on the sum of £9 required to "waft him to the torrid zone" but sometimes employers abroad were willing to "indent" or subsidize employees, recovering their advance from the first year's salary. Friends were urging him to gather his poems together for publication to provide the necessary funds and, after despatching another note to Richmond — "My hour is come — you and I will never meet in Britain more. I have orders within three weeks at farthest to repair aboard the *Nancy* — Captain Smith — from Clyde to Jamaica, calling at Antigua" — he began to entertain these suggestions seriously.

From time to time he received word from James Smith who was Jean's confidant too, that she still loved him in spite of appearances to the contrary, but it was now too late to reverse his plans and his pride had been dealt a mortal blow by her unexpected betrayal. "I need not tell you that the receipt of your last letter gave me pleasure," he wrote Smith and added a quatrain that revealed the true state of his feelings:

> O, Jenny, thou hast stolen away my soul!
> In vain I strive against the lov'd idea:
> Thy tender image sallies on my thoughts
> My firm resolves become an easy prey!

At the same time he impressed upon Smith that there could be no last-minute reconciliation with Jean. The die was cast. "Against two things I am fixed as fate: staying at home and owning her conjugally," he told Smith. "The first, by Heaven I will not do! The last, by Hell, I will never do!" Besides, Mary Campbell, who had sympathized with him deeply during the period of his repudiation by the Armours, now stood between himself and Jean. Mary had given herself to him. He could not betray her trust. If Jean did not want him — as her conduct had demonstrated — Mary did. She had arranged to leave her employment in Mauchline and to return to her parents' home in the West Highlands before going on to Glasgow where she would enter domestic service in the home of a Colonel McIvor. There she would wait until Robert was in a position to send for her.

Before leaving the country Robert decided to take a last revenge on the detestable Armours. He intended to turn over his own interest in the farming venture at Mossgiel to his brother Gilbert, in which case there would be no personal assets for old Armour to recover in the matter of the writ. Accordingly, he arranged to have his action legally "cried" three times at the market Cross in Ayr — a published proceeding that made the matter formal:

> Know all men by these presents that I, Robert Burns in Mossgiel: whereas I intend to go abroad and, having acknowledged myself the father of a child named Elizabeth begot upon Elizabeth Paton of Largieside: and whereas Gilbert Burns in Mossgiel, my brother, has become bound, and hereby binds and obligates himself to aliment, clothe and educate my said natural child in a suitable manner as if she was his own, in case her Mother choose to part with her; and that, until she arrive at the age of fifteen. . . .

At the age of fifteen she would enter domestic service under the eye of a watchful and benevolent employer. By that time, baby Bess would be old enough for launching on an independent career during the years preceding marriage to a likely young man and Gilbert's responsibilities would be ended. Everything was arranged for Lizzie Paton's child — nothing for Jean Armour's coming offspring! Let the Armours digest this dig! And Robert also arranged that, after his poems were published, baby Bess would possess their copyright, too.

He had heard that Jean was being deserted by many of her former friends and that she was enduring certain indignities at home: that when her father read the customary bible chapter at the breakfast table on Sundays, she was requested to leave the room and that she knelt by herself during family prayers in the parlour in the evening. He thought of her constantly just now — preparing forlornly for her coming ordeal and snubbed by those whose protection was her right and he lashed out in a bitter denunciation of her accusers in a poem entitled *Address to the Unco Guid or Rigidly Righteous*:

> O ye who are sae guid yoursel',
>   Sae pious an' sae holy,
> Ye've nought to do but mark an' tell
>   Your neighbour's faults and folly. . . .
>
> Ye high, exalted, virtuous dames,
>   Tied up in godly laces,
> Before ye gie poor Frailty names,
>   Suppose a change o' cases;
>
> A dear-loved lad, convenience snug —
>   A treacherous inclination —
> But let me whisper in your lug
>   *Ye're* maybe nae temptation!

Its final stanza, pregnant with an eloquent plea for compassion and understanding, was to endure for centuries to come:

> Who made the heart, 'tis He alone
>   Decidedly can try us;
> He knows each chord — its various tone
>   Each spring — its various bias:
> Then at the balance let's be mute,
>   We never can adjust it;

> What's done we *partly* may compute
> But know not what's resisted.

Deeply moved by the plea, Wordsworth was to write later: "The momentous truth of this passage could not possibly have been conveyed with such pathetic force by any poet that ever lived, speaking in his own voice; unless it were felt that, like Burns, he was a man who preached from the text of his own errors; and whose wisdom was in fact a scion from the root of personal suffering."

CHAPTER 5

On the second Sunday in May — not long after Robert had confided to his friends Brice, Smith and Richmond his plans for going abroad — he had bid farewell to Mary in a dramatic mood. They had stood on either side of a small purling stream known as the Fail, joining hands beneath its waters to cement their vows to each other in traditional style. To add solemnity to the occasion, they had also exchanged bibles. The bible Mary gave Robert has never been found but the two-volume bible Robert gave to her is now to be seen in the museum of the Burns Monument in Alloway. On the fly-leaf of the first volume Robert inscribed: "And ye shall not swear by my Name falsely, neither shalt thou profane the name of thy God: I am the Lord. Levit. 19th chap., verse 12" and, in the other volume: "Thou shalt not forswear thyself but shalt perform unto the Lord thine oaths. Matth. 5th, verse 33." In both bibles he wrote his signature "Robert Burns, Mossgiel" and appended his Masonic mark. The texts had been chosen by Robert deliberately. Mary would be able to show the bibles to her parents who were simple, God-fearing folks and, knowing nothing of his legal involvement with another young woman in Ayrshire, would be glad to accept his Holy Writ pledges to their Mary.

Robert was singularly guarded concerning his relations with the girl he had named "Highland Mary" because she had come from an area where Gaelic was the common tongue. It is possible that, in his heart of hearts, he may well have doubted whether or not the destruction of the "marriage lines" he had given to Jean rendered them invalid should anyone be interested enough to resurrect them. He may also have realized that gossip concerning his alleged relations with Mary Campbell at this particular time was likely to reflect little credit upon him and perhaps he feared an accusation of bigamy later on should old Armour prove vindictive. In later years — when there was then no further need for caution — he was to confess to a friend that there had been "a pretty long tract of the most ardent reciprocal attachment" between himself and Mary and that she had been "a warm-hearted and charming young creature as ever blessed a man with generous love." To a man as sexually driven as Burns, "generous love" and "most ardent reciprocal attachment" could only reflect one interpretation.

Mary Campbell was twenty-three when she met Robert for the first time in Ayrshire. It was related that her father was a sailor on a revenue-cutter during the smuggling days on the West coast; that, one of a sizeable family of boys and girls, she had spent some of her early days in the home of the reverend David Campbell of Loch Ranza who was a relation of her mother; and that she had come to Ayrshire to seek domestic employment at the suggestion of a relative who held a house-keeper's position there.

Authorities have differed widely on the subject of Mary Campbell's charms — or lack of them. We are told, on the one hand, that she was "a sweet, sprightly, blue-eyed, golden-haired creature who was a paragon of goodness and girlish innocence" and, on the other, that she was "not endowed with a fraction of the sweet, indefinite attractions with which Burns invested her." There was a tradition in the Burns country, declared one historian, that she was "neither graceful nor feminine but was a coarse-featured, ungainly country lass" and it is well to remember the comment of his own brother that Robert was inclined to invest his charmers with imagined virtues "out of the plentiful stores of his own imagination." Be that as it may — and no portrait of Mary Campbell has come down to posterity to settle the matter — Mary had one out-standing virtue — constancy and devotion to Robert which inspired a poetic tribute in her honour:

> Altho' thro' foreign climes I range,
> I know her heart will never change,
> For her bosom burns with honour's glow,
> My faithful Highland lassie, O.
>
> For her I'll dare the billows' roar,
> For her I'll trace a distant shore,
> That Indian wealth may lustre throw
> Around my Highland lassie, O.
>
> She has my heart, she has my hand
> By sacred troth and honour's band!
> Till mortal stroke shall lay me low,
> I'm thine, my Highland lassie, O.

With Mary now gone to her parents in Campbeltown to announce her betrothal and Jean permanently inaccessible, Robert set about carrying his poems piecemeal to a printer called Wilson in the town of Kilmarnock who agreed to print six hundred copies "elegantly printed in one volume octavo at a price, stitched, of Three Shillings." Resplendent in blue board covers (with white back), the volume containing forty-four poems, appeared on the last day of July and Robert confided to a friend that he "felt pretty confident his *Poems* would meet with applause." It was a prophecy that was to be amply vindicated in the days that lay ahead. "The *Poems* were received with favour, even with rapture, in Ayrshire and, before long, in the adjoining shires," wrote a reporter. "Old and young, high and low, grave and gay, learned or ignorant, were alike delighted, agitated, transported . . . even ploughboys and maidservants would gladly have spent the wages they earned most hardly and which they needed to purchase necessary clothing, if they might but procure the *Poems* of Burns." Loyal and enthusiastic friends began to beat the drums loudly in Robert's behalf and the subscription lists mushroomed. By the end of August only fifteen copies remained and these had been spoken for many times over. In spite of his professional friendship with Armour, lawyer Aiken of Ayr ordered 145 copies; James Smith of Mauchline 70 and Gavin Hamilton at least 40. Robert Muir, wine merchant in Kilmarnock spoke for 72 copies and printer Wilson himself disposed of 70 copies and could have doubled this number had copies been available. Gilbert, delighted by his brother's achievement, stretched his limited purse to the utmost to obtain copies and, additionally, orders came in from much further afield — from David Sillar of Irvine, William Niven of Maybole, Walter Morton of Cumnock, John Rankine of Adamhill, John Neilson, William Parker, John Kennedy, Ralph Sellars and many others. By the time all orders were filled, Robert could not even find a copy for his own mother and sisters.

By degrees the *Poems* found their way into distinguished circles. Mrs. Frances Dunlop of Dunlop, daughter of Sir William Wallace, collateral descendant of the famous Wallace who had burned the barns of Ayr, received a copy of them while she was recovering from a long illness and was enchanted with them — especially with *The Cotter's Saturday Night*. She sent a letter to Robert at Mossgiel requesting half a dozen copies of the *Poems* and invited him to visit her personally at her country Dower House. Posing as an antiquarian, eager to encourage efforts to enhance Scotland's traditions, she had greatly enjoyed the flavour of Robert's poems though, inclined to be prim and conventional in spite of having brought into the world and reared a large family of children, she later upbraided her *protégé* claiming that some of the poems and songs in lighter vein left something to be desired in the matter of delicacy.

News of Burns's achievement spread rapidly beyond the borders of Ayrshire and the gentry "began to notice Mr. Burns with polite and friendly attention." Riding over to the parish of Loudoun to bid farewell to its minister the reverend George Lawrie, he learned that the cleric had sent a copy of the *Poems* to the celebrated Doctor Blacklock of Edinburgh, requesting that they be brought to the attention of "those whose critical judgment was sound and whose influence might be helpful in procuring a living for their author at home." It would be a pity if Scotland's talented son should be lost to the country. Doctor Blacklock had taken his time in replying to Lawrie's letter but when he did so he related he had already heard of the *Poems* through Professor Dugald Stewart, friend of Dr. John Mackenzie who had read them in manuscript form. He promised, however, that should the author decide to visit Edinburgh — and a large second edition of the *Poems* was being mooted — he would introduce him to the reverend Doctor Blair, author of several books on religious themes, who was regarded as the *doyen* of the city's literary circles. The reverend Doctor had already proclaimed the *Poems* "the work of a very fine genius."

Flattering invitations from the elite now began to pour in on him. Attired in his Sunday best, he had "spreckl'd o'er the brae" to dine with the young and affable Lord Daer and the social attentions he received made him take another look at precipitate plans for going abroad. Another edition of the *Poems* — three thousand copies at least — was being urged upon him by Ayrshire friends, but the Kilmarnock printer who had printed the first one declined to handle a second printing unless paid in advance for the paper required, and he was too proud to accept the offer of an Ayrshire friend to advance the money. Influential acquaintances in Edinburgh urged him to seek another publisher and promised the help of well-disposed Freemasons there.

He had received discouraging reports of life in far-off Jamaica. Travellers, recently returned from the West Indies, had warned him it might be better to postpone his sailing to a later date, embarking on a vessel called the *Nancy* which would take him straight to his final destination instead of landing him at a port called Savannah-la-Mar entailing an overland journey at the risk of suffering "a pleuritic fever while travelling in the hot sun." He had discussed the matter with Gavin Hamilton, whose friend, a Captain Cathcart, skippered the *Nancy* which was due to sail in September. If he delayed his departure until then he would be able to help Gilbert harvest the crops at Mossgiel. Captain Cathcart of the *Nancy* was "as good a fellow as heart could wish," Robert wrote a friend. "With him I am destined to go." But Jamaica did not now appear to be the rosy haven he had fondly imagined it to be. He had recently received a letter from a John Hutchinson, a casual acquaintance there, who, in acknowledging receipt of a complimentary copy of the *Poems,* had declared: "I have great reason to think Dr. Douglas's employ would by no means answer your expectations . . . I can by no means advise you to think of coming to the West Indies as I assure you there is no encouragement for a man of learning and genius here; and am very confident you can do far better in Great Britain than in Jamaica. . . ."

Thanks to Robert's new-won fame and to the intervention of influential friends, James Armour had been persuaded to withdraw the writ against him and efforts were being made to find employment for him at home — possibly in the Excise service due to his knowledge of mensuration acquired in earlier days in Kilmarnock. Jean's child would be born early in September and his concern for her was mounting. He wrote John Richmond:

> I am in little apprehension now about Armour. The warrant is still in existence but some of the first gentlemen in the country have offered to befriend me and, besides, Jean will not take any step against me without letting me know, as nothing but the most violent menaces could have forced her to sign the petition. I have called on her once and again of late; as she is, at this moment, threatened with the pangs of travail; and I assure you, my dear friend, I cannot help being anxious — very anxious — for her situation. She would gladly now embrace that offer she once rejected, but it shall never more be in her power. . . .

It was not that he had ceased to love Jean entirely; but that Mary Campbell, waiting trustfully for him in the West country and possibly in grave need of his assurances, now stood inexorably between them and by now the last of his bridges had been burned. On the eve of his anticipated emigration he had composed a poem that reflected his true thoughts concerning Jean and her plight and his inability to reverse the wheels that were propelling him abroad:

> Farewell, old Scotia's bleak domains
> Far dearer than the torrid plains
> Where rich ananas blow!
> Farewell, a mother's blessing dear!
> A brother's sigh! A sister's tear!
> My Jean's heartrending throe!
>
> Farewell, my Bess, tho' thou'rt bereft
> Of my parental care;
> A faithful brother I have left
> My part in him you'll share;
> Adieu, too, to you, too —
> My Smith, my bosom friend!
> When kindly you remember me
> O, then befriend my Jean!
>
> What bursting anguish tears my heart!
> From thee, my Jeanie, must I part?
> Thou, weeping, answer'st "No!"
> Alas! misfortune stares my face
> And points to ruin and disgrace;
> I for thy sake must go. . . .

"Ruin and disgrace?" Was there now some new emergency that had embroiled him? The Armour disgrace was by now an open secret and could scarcely have justified his distracted confession to a correspondent:

I have been for some time pining under secret wretchedness, from causes which you pretty well know — the pang of disappointment, the sting of pride, with some wandering stabs of remorse which never fail to settle my vitals like vultures when attention is not called away by the calls of society or the vagaries of the Muse. Even in the hour of social mirth, my gaiety is the madness of an intoxicated criminal under the hands of the executioner.

Some biographers, struck with the intensity of his desperation, have contended that Mary Campbell as well as Jean Armour was pregnant at this time which might account for his deliberate secrecy regarding his relations with Gavin Hamilton's young nursemaid but their assumptions have never been substantiated. In a fragmentary Song entitled *My Jean* he still mourned the circumstances that were parting them:

> Though cruel fate should bid us part
>   Far as the pole and line;
> Her dear idea round my heart
>   Should tenderly entwine.
> Tho' mountains frown and deserts howl
>   And oceans roar between;
> Yet dearer than my deathless soul
>   I still would love my Jean

but, almost in the same breath, he paid loving tribute to the patiently waiting Mary:

> Will ye go to the Indies, my Mary,
>   And leave auld Scotia's shore?
> Will ye go to the Indies, my Mary
>   Across the Atlantic's roar? . . .
>
> I hae sworn by the Heavens to my Mary,
>   I hae sworn by the Heavens to be true;
> And may the Heavens forget me
>   When I forget my vow! . .
>
> We hae plighted our troth, my Mary,
>   In mutual affection to join;
> And curst be the cause that shall part us!
>   The hour and the moment of time!

The more Robert reflected on his present situation, however, the more he felt disposed to head for Edinburgh where a new world and environment might serve to dissipate his torments. Jean was out of his life — presumably forever — Mary Campbell had left the parish and Lizzie Paton, convinced that he had made a tidy fortune out of his *Poems* was suing him for maternity subsidy. What had he to lose by shaking the clay of rural Ayrshire off his restless feet?

Day after day, week after week, however, he lingered in Mauchline as if rooted to the spot. In the secret places of his heart he longed to hold Jean's child in his arms and he cherished a hope that the miracle of a first grandchild might soften the hearts of the recalcitrant Armours.

On Sunday, the third day of September, when he was busy in the barn, Jean's younger brother Adam arrived breathless at Mossgiel with some momentous news. Jean had been bedded. Doctor Mackenzie and the village midwife were in close attendance while Mary Armour hovered maternally in the background to lend an experienced hand.

An access of unbearable joy swept over Robert. Hastily saddling his pony, he dug his heels impatiently into its flanks and turned its nose towards the village, stopping en route at the home of Gavin Hamilton to persuade John Blane, his former ploughboy now in more profitable employment as a messenger for the lawyer, to accompany him to the Armour home in the Cowgate. The accommodating Blane agreed readily enough and reported to his employer afterwards that they had been "received with all civility" and had been allowed to go upstairs to the room in which Jean, her ordeal over, lay happily spent. Recorded Blane graphically:

> Jean held up a pretty female infant to Burns who took it in his arms and, after keeping it a little while, returned it to the mother, asking the blessing of God Almighty on her and her infant. Burns was turning away to converse with others in the room when Jean said archly: "But this is not all — here is another baby!" and handed him a male child that had been born at the same time. He was greatly surprised but took that child, too, into his arms and repeated his blessing upon it. His melancholy mood then changed to the mirthful and our visit was concluded by his giving Jean Armour a hearty caress and teasing her on this promising beginning of her history as a mother. . . .

The floodgates of emotion that had churned within him for many a month burst suddenly and, tears coursing unrestrained down his cheeks, Robert rode back to Mossgiel with new hope in his heart though the mason had escorted him to the door coldly and had closed it resolutely behind him. There would be time enough, he informed Robert, for further parleying when wishful thinking had been translated into practical reality — a reality of ready cash which would enable him to assume his new parental responsibilities and set up a way of life that would recommend him to respectable society. Resumption of his former relations with Jean was unthinkable, he insisted. It could only lead to a repetition of what had gone before. Besides, it would only unsettle Jean at a time when clear, unemotional reflection was imperative.

The infants were christened Robert and Jean and their father penned a jubilant note to John Richmond in Edinburgh:

> Wish me luck, my dear Richmond! Armour has just brought me a fine boy and girl at one throw. God bless the little dears!

and he tossed off a lighthearted quatrain for full measure:

> Green grow the rashes, O,
> Green grow the rashes, O;
> A feather bed is no sae saft
> As the bosoms of the lasses, O!

To his friend Robert Muir, wine merchant in Kilmarnock and boon companion of many a convivial carousal at the inn there, he wrote:

> You will have heard that poor Armour has repaid my amorous mortgages double. A very fine boy and girl have awakened a thousand tender feelings that thrill, some with tender pressure and some with foreboding anguish through my soul. . . .

Muir was a family man and would understand the feelings that wracked him. He also composed for Gavin Hamilton — to celebrate his dual paternity — a long *double entendre* poem entitled *Nature's Law*:

> A hero of these artless strains
>   A lowly bard was he,
> Who sang his rhymes in Coila's plains
>   With meikle mirth and glee.
> Kind Nature's care had given his share
>   Large of the flaming current;
> And, all devout, he never sought
>   To stem the sacred torrent.
>
> He felt the powerful high behest
>   Thrill vital thro' and thro';
> And sought a correspondent breast
>   To give obedience due;
> Propitious pow'rs screen'd the young flow'rs
>   From mildews of abortion;
> And lo! — the bard — a great reward
>   Has got a *double* portion! . .

Day after day, riding about the shire collecting monies still owing to him for copies of his *Poems,* he waited anxiously for some sign of capitulation from the Armour camp but none came and he was convinced that James and Mary Armour were deliberately circumventing his messages to Jean through an intermediary. Chafing under suspense one day, he hailed a horseback carrier who was passing the gates of Mossgiel on the way to the village, requesting him to convey "some delicacies of the farm to his poor wife in Mauchline." John Kennedy, long a sympathizer of Burns, agreed willingly, reporting afterwards that Mary Armour, her hackles rising visibly, had opened the door to him and denounced him loudly for being a friend of such a scamp as Burns of Mossgiel. Hearing the commotion at the door, it appeared, mason Armour had intervened, permitting Kennedy to go upstairs to deliver the basket to Jean. He had not been long in the room, he declared, when he heard a scuffling on the stairs and Robert himself — hatless and distraught — had burst into the room followed by the panting Armours who had "exhausted their strength in trying to repel him." Rushing to Jean's side, Robert had put his cheek to hers and, in turn, to those of the sleeping infants and he had wept bitterly. Unmoved by the poignant scene, however, the Armours had ushered him down the stairs and out into the street where a knot of curious townsfolk, attracted by the noise, had gathered silently.

September gave way to October. The harvest was in and still another vessel had sailed to the West Indies without him and at the end of the month Robert received a letter in an unfamiliar hand advising that Mary Campbell had died unexpectedly and mysteriously in Greenock where she had been visiting relatives prior to going to Glasgow. She had been buried with scant ceremony in the Old West Churchyard about the middle of the month and although it was known that, during her visit there, a plague raged in the town and that she had nursed a young relative who was stricken, ugly rumours reared their head and eyebrows were raised significantly. She was reported to have caught "the fever" but there were fevers and fevers and she had left Ayrshire in the best of health and in the prime of her days. The facts seemed suspicious when it was learned she had recently become betrothed to Robert Burns of Mauchline. Robert added little to the score though his sisters had noted that when he read the letter containing the news he had turned on his heels and left the room, his face contorted with some private agony. To a new poem entitled *My Highland Lassie* forwarded to his publisher he added an explanatory note that the subject of the song had "crossed the sea to meet him at Greenock where she had scarce landed when she was seized with a malignant fever which hurried my dear girl to her grave in a few days, before I could even hear of her illness."

Rumours of Robert's reputed relations with Mary Campbell persisted, however, and it was reported that the men of the Campbell clan had given orders that the name of Robert Burns was never to be mentioned in their hearing again and it was discovered later on that part of the inscription in the bible he had given Mary had been expunged by what seemed a deliberate wet thumb. Was it the thumb of Mary herself, some asked, disappointed and disillusioned by his failure to implement his vows? And at what might have been a particularly critical time? What reason could he have had, argued others, for lingering indefinitely in Ayrshire long after Jean's offspring had been born if it were not that he had decided to jettison Mary who was now out of sight and presumably out of mind too? There was no answer to these riddles, it seemed, but later on, when he was by then a happily married man, he was to pour out his grief in an exquisite poem composed on the anniversary of Highland Mary's death:

> That sacred hour can I forget
>   Can I forget the hallowed grove
> Where by the winding Ayr we met
>   To live one day of parting love!
> Eternity will not efface
>   Those records dear of transports past;
> Thy image at our last embrace;
>   Ah! little thought we 'twas our last.
>
> Still fondly o'er these scenes my mem'ry wakes
>   And fondly broods with miser care!
> Time but the impression deeper makes

As streams their channels deeper wear.
My Mary, dear departed shade!
   Where is thy place of blissful rest?
See'st thou thy lover lowly laid?
   Hear'st thou the groans that rend his breast?

Time was to add little to the record of Robert's love for Mary Campbell and the circumstances of her untimely death. Her life-sized statue overlooking the harbour of Dunoon on the River Clyde is mute and the bronze effigy of Burns and Highland Mary in Beacon Hill Park in the capital city of British Columbia records only the sunny hours they knew in its moving inscription once penned by Burns in a retrospective mood:

The golden hours on angel-wings
Flew o'er me and my dearie;
For dear to me as light and life
Was my sweet Highland Mary

The sudden and unexpected death of Mary Campbell, painful as it was to Robert, must, in certain respects, have seemed providential. It had eliminated threat of trouble with her relatives should they discover his legal embroilment with Jean and, if he went ahead with plans for marrying Mary, a more serious charge of bigamy. The death of Mary Campbell removed a number of other hazardous gambits on his cluttered checkerboard and now he felt doubly inclined to accept the persuasions of his Edinburgh admirers. Alexander Dalziel, factor of the Renfrewshire estates of the Earl of Glencairn, had written informing him that he had sent a copy of the *Poems* to the young Earl who had been delighted with them and intended having them "richly bound for his library." Moreover, the Earl wished sincerely to befriend him. The Earl, who was a prominent Freemason, offered to introduce him to William Creech, former tutor to his brother, who had now turned publisher and had published the works of many prominent Edinburgh *literateurs.* Publisher Creech's fashionable *levees,* held on his business premises, attracted men of rank, culture and influence, and the Earl himself was a member of the exclusive Caledonian Hunt Club whose members might subscribe generously to the new edition.

Finally a decision was made for Gilbert had offered to keep a fraternal eye on matters at Mossgiel, on the health and welfare of baby Bess now flourishing under the maternal care of Agnes Burns and on matters relating to Jean and her infants.

On the 27th of November, when the hedgerows were jewelled with scarlet berries and a delicate tracery of hoar-frost spangled the fields, Robert set out for Edinburgh on a pony borrowed from a farmer friend which was to be returned to its owner in due course. He arrived in the capital city a couple of days later and proceeded to the lodgings of John Richmond in Baxter's Close which he was to share with his friend for a modest three shillings a week. He would be free to come and go as he pleased, Richmond had assured him, though they would be sharing the same bed in a large ground-floor room of a house owned by a Mrs. Carfrae, a respectable widow of temperate habits and middle-aged tolerance.

Exhausted by the sixty-mile ride from Mauchline and by the convivial hospitality that had been extended to him en route and "a miserable headache and a stomach ailment," he spent the first few days in Edinburgh taking things easy until he felt equal to sightseeing. He wandered about the city leisurely, feasting his eyes upon the smoke-wreathed horizons of the old town from the eminence of King Arthur's Seat and on the battle-scarred ramparts of the ancient Castle. He was fascinated by the well-supplied booksellers' shops in the High Street though his own *Poems* had not yet appeared in their windows. And, later, by candlelight in Richmond's lodgings, he tried his hand at a poetic *Address to Edinburgh* in which he lauded its hoary traditions, its famous halls of learning, its wealth and classic architecture, the beauty of its women and the cordiality of its men. Expecting that he would soon be invited to the tables of eminent hosts, he had himself measured for new clothes — the fashionable Fox livery worn in *haute monde* circles, consisting of a blue coat with metal buttons, a yellow and blue striped waistcoat, a fine white cambric neckcloth, the tightest of buckskins and glossy top boots.

He wandered into the Old Cannongate churchyard in search of the grave of his predecessor, the poet Fergusson, and, finding it neglected and unmarked, knelt down and reverently kissed its sod, resolving to purchase a tombstone for it; and he visited the old house in which Allan Ramsay, author of his favourite poem, *The Gentle Shepherd,* had once lived and, entering it, removed his hat in respectful tribute to a fellow-craftsman.

He was in no particular hurry to avail himself of an introduction he carried in his pocket from Ayrshire and the invitations that were left for him at the lodgings in Baxter's Close. He preferred to wait until, suitably attired for the salons of the elite, he might appear creditably among them and when he did so his appearance and deportment electrified them. His jet black hair, without the customary powder, was tied at the nape of the neck and spread neatly upon his forehead, reported the local news-sheets. To critical observers his deportment was "modest and becoming" and, free of the timidity and reticence they had expected, he "took part in social conversation with freedom and energy but without the least forwardness." The wives and daughters of his hosts described his conversation as fascinating and it was reported that he "addressed them with special deference." The unconventional Duchess of Gordon who had obtained her title by a fortuitous social marriage and was notorious for mingling with dubious company in the popular oyster-cellars of the town and seldom retired to bed before dawn, declared she had never met a man whose "conversation so carried her off her feet" and she had met many interesting men in her time; while socialite Alison Cockburn, writing to a distant friend, related: "The town is, at present, agog with the Ploughman Poet. He receives adulation with native dignity and is the very figure of his profession."

Expecting to welcome a burly, stoop-shouldered son of toil, the clay of rural Ayrshire splashed liberally on his top boots and a thick Doric burr on his tongue, his hosts were surprised and even a little deflated to discover that Ploughman Burns was no dolt and was well able to hold his own among them. And Principal Robertson, a frequent guest at the breakfast table of the eccentric legal luminary, Lord Monboddo, declared he "had scarcely met a man whose conversation displayed greater vigour" — and, he, too, had met famous men in his time.

Wishing to ingratiate himself with the old Earl, Robert composed a poetic tribute to the charms of his young daughter — "Heavenly Burnet" — and told friends in Ayrshire "there has not been anything like her in all the combinations of beauty, grace and goodness the Great Creator has formed since Milton's Eve." To Robert she was a new kind of female, though his passionate admiration of her charms may well have been inspired by her father's ruby port for we are told that she was a pale, languid young creature with bad teeth and she died shortly afterwards of "a galloping consumption."

Reviewing the first Kilmarnock edition of the *Poems,* Edinburgh journalists stressed their author's origin as a "Heaven-inspired Ploughman" and, while Robert evinced little desire to pose as a *rara avis* with plebeian feathers, he was shrewd enough to assess the value of such a provocative image. The December issue of *The Lounger,* edited by Henry Mackenzie, carried a somewhat patronizing review of his work and origin:

> . . . In mentioning the circumstances of his humble station, I mean not to rest his pretensions solely on that title, or to urge the merits of his poetry when considered in relation to the lowness of his birth and the little opportunity which his education could afford. These particulars, indeed, might excite our wonder at his productions; but his poetry, considered abstractedly and without the apologies arising from his situation, seem to me fully entitled to command our feelings and to obtain our applause. . . .

It was a grudging and snobbish critique and one that must have made the author wince. The "lowness of his birth" stigma was in direct contravention of the social conversation he exhibited — larded with elegant French phrases and Latin tags — proclaiming that he was by no means a cloddish uneducated man. He was willing to pocket his pride, however, for the sake of the acclaim he hoped his second edition (containing many new poems) would win.

Exception was also taken by critic Henry Mackenzie to the Doric dialect in which most of his poems were written since, after the Union of the Crowns in 1707, the Scots tongue had become considerably anglicized in polite circles. Complained Mackenzie:

> . . . One bar, indeed, his birth and education have opposed to his fame
> — the language in which many of his poems are written. Even in
> Scotland, the provincial dialect which Ramsay and he have used is
> now read with a difficulty which greatly damps the pleasure of the
> reader; in England it cannot be read at all, without such a constant
> reference to a glossary as nearly to destroy the pleasure. . . .

A frequent guest in the well-appointed homes of his new patrons, Robert found the somewhat pedestrian lodgings he shared with Richmond a little deflating but his friend was kind and considerate, helping him to prepare his new poems for publication and reading to him until he fell asleep after returning past midnight, flushed, feverish and heated with wine. The prevailing drinking habits of his hosts in Edinburgh "took a heavy slice of his constitution," he told his rural friends but he was anxious to appear among them as a man who could meet their manly capacity. He dreaded the customary *Round of Toasts* after the ladies had left the table. Each gentleman was required to propose a clever or a witty toast, to which each of the other guests in turn made an equally scintillating response. At a dinner party of ten guests, therefore, the glass was raised to the lips a hundred times — and then it was time for another *Round* to begin. Flunkeys moved in discreetly with relieving vessels and the tipsy guests edged themselves out of the dining room by clinging to the wainscotting.

In subsequent letters home Robert complained that Richmond's economical quarters were anything but restful and that he frequently suffered from lack of sleep. Mrs. Carfrae, their landlady — "a staid, sober, piously-disposed, evil-abhorring widow" (approaching the change of life, confided Robert) was "in sore tribulation" concerning some Daughters of Belial who occupied the floor above." Explained Robert: "Our floors are ill-plastered and so low that we can easily distinguish when our laughter-loving, night rejoicing neighbours are eating, when they are drinking and when they are, Etc." Poor, respectable Mrs. Carfrae "tossed sleepless and unquiet, looking for rest and finding none, the whole night through." She had developed a comfortable philosophy, however. "Heaven would take care of these Daughters of Belial," she assured Richmond and Robert. "We need not be uneasy because the wicked enjoy the good things of life, for these base jades who lie up gandygoin' with their filthy fellows — drinking the best of wines and singing abominable songs — will one day lie in Hell, weeping and wailing and gnashing their teeth over a cup of God's wrath!" But times were hard, the Daughters of Belial paid well and they were allowed to stay while good Mrs. Carfrae wrestled with the Devil for their souls in St. Giles Cathedral on a Sunday.

Robert's letters home were full of his conquests and new social successes in Edinburgh. The Earl of Glencairn and Mr. Erskine, distinguished Dean of the Law Faculty, had "taken him under their wing," he told them and "invitations were being showered upon him as thick and fast as visiting cards," he told Hamilton. "In all probability I shall soon be the tenth Worthy and the eighth Wise Man of the world. I am in a fair way of becoming as eminent as Thomas à Kempis or John Bunyan and you may expect henceforth to see my birthday inserted among the wonderful events in the Poor Robin and Aberdeen Almanacks, with Black Monday and the Battle of Bothwell Bridge."

Pecuniary necessity uppermost in his mind, he determined to dedicate the new edition of the *Poems* to the wealthy and influential Gentlemen of the Caledonian Hunt and, hearing of this graceful gesture, the Earl of Glencairn had made a motion at a Masonic meeting that, "in consideration of Mr. Burns's superior merit, as well as of the compliment he did them, the treasurer should be authorized to subscribe in their name for one hundred copies of the published volume for which Mr. Burns should be paid the sum of twenty-five pounds."

To his Ayrshire friend Ballantine, who had previously offered to lend him the money to launch the second edition, Robert waxed enthusiastic about his new patrons — a galaxy of stars in the city's brightest legal, cultural and literary firmament. "I have some warm friends among the *literati*," he boasted — "Professors Stewart, Blair, Mackenzie and others." An anonymous well-wisher (who turned out to be Patrick Miller, brother of the eminent Justice Clerk and who was to become Robert's landlord later on when he returned to farming in Dumfriesshire) left a handsome gift of ten guineas for the Bard with Sibbald, an Edinburgh bookseller, and the Earl of Glencairn sent a number of subscription forms for the new volume to the Marquis of Graham with a request that they be "filled up with all the first Scottish names about Court." Lord Eglinton, Governor of Edinburgh Castle and a former member of Parliament, sent ten guineas for a brace of volumes and Robert was invited to take breakfast with Lord Maitland and some of his friends. His early Masonic associations in Tarbolton and later in Mauchline stood him in good stead. They ensured him immediate acceptance in the social circles he was now frequenting. Soon after his arrival in the city he had attended a meeting of the Grand Lodge of Scotland and its Most Worshipful Master had raised a toast to "Caledonia and Caledonia's Bard, Brother Burns," to which Robert had replied making an excellent impression upon those present. "The meeting was numerous and elegant," he wrote Ballantine, "and all the Lodges about town were present in all their pomp." It was a signal tribute to an unlettered rustic ploughman!

The village of Mauchline and all its concerns now seemed very far away but Gavin Hamilton kept him up-to-date on happenings there and sent him what little news there was to relate about Jean and the Armour family and Robert confessed nostalgically "To tell you the truth among friends, I feel a miserable blank in my heart for want of her and I don't think I shall ever meet with so delicious an armful again. She has her faults; and so have you and I, and so has everybody else" and he appended a light-hearted stanza:

Their tricks an' craft hae put me daft
They've ta'en me in an' a' that;
But clear the decks and here's "The Sex!"
I like the jades for a' that. . . .

He had not forgotten his sweet, yielding Jean in Ayrshire but the heady excitements of his new life in Edinburgh and the many miles that separated them were gradually dimming her bright image. Gilbert kept him informed about the family troubles at Mossgiel and about the health and lispings of baby Bess. Agnes Burns and their sisters were working harder than ever in the dairy to increase production of the sweet milk cheeses for which they found a ready market, but Hamilton's rent was still badly in arrears and they naturally looked to successful Robert for a measure of financial aid. He had never failed them in the past and, expecting him to make a fortune out of the new edition of his *Poems,* they counted on his help in the future. Hamilton, too, was heartened by Robert's new prospects and asked him to sign a document guaranteeing financial assistance to Gilbert to enable him to wipe out arrears of rent but Robert, painfully apologetic, had felt obliged to refuse the request at a somewhat uncertain stage in his affairs. Like everyone else, Gavin Hamilton would have to wait until more cash jingled in his pockets. Robert was far too proud to beg the favour of loans from his Edinburgh patrons. Moreover, he felt unable to predict how long his meteoric popularity was likely to last. Shrewd enough to realise that he was now on the crest of the wave and that his popularity was likely to wane once the *haute monde* of Edinburgh had sated its curiosity about him, he knew it was only a matter of time before he would have to return to what he described as his "rural shades." Nor, strangely enough, did the prospect dismay him. Many of his letters home revealed a secret yearning to return to the soil that had nourished his forebears and to enjoy once again the rugged hospitality of the convivial country inns and the stimulating society of men of his own hardy breed. After a prolonged period in the hothouse *milieu* of Edinburgh he had few illusions about the tenuous quality of the acclaim he had won. Frances Dunlop, who was still corresponding with him in the guise of a mother-confessor, had cautioned him anxiously that his sudden fame must not be allowed to turn his head and he had replied:

You are afraid that I shall grow intoxicated with my prosperity as a Poet: alas, Madam, I know myself and the world too well. I am willing to believe that my abilities deserve some notice but in a most enlightened age when poetry has been the study of men of the first genius, to be dragged forth to the full glare of polite observation, with all my imperfections of awkward rusticity and crude, unpolished ideas — I assure you, Madam, I do not dissemble when I tell you I tremble for the consequences . . . and too surely do I see the time when such a tide will surely leave me . . . and when it recedes you will bear me witness that, when my bubble of fame was at its highest, I stood unintoxicated with the inebriating cup in my hand and anticipated the time when calumny should dash it to the ground. . . .

Calumny was already rearing its ugly head. He had been accused of unforgivable *faux pas* at the tables of his well-born hosts; of giving offence to his "betters" in their salons and of frequenting second-rate taverns thronged by men of his own plebeian stripe and, most unforgivable of all, of "showing a new arrogance in conversation" at social gatherings. It was an arrogance, however, that was personally protective. He deeply resented the condescending patronage of his hosts and their exploitation; and their ungenerous insinuation that lack of formal education stamped him as an inferior being. What his critics probably resented most of all, he believed, was that the "Heaven-inspired Ploughman," the "Inspired Faun," was not the ignoramus they had deemed him to be. An entry in his second Commonplace Book (started to reveal his Edinburgh impressions) revealed his chagrin:

> There are few of the sore evils under the sun give me more uneasiness and chagrin than the comparison how a man of Genius and avowed worth is everywhere received with the reception which a mere ordinary character — decorated with the trappings and distinctions of Fortune — meets. Imagine a man of abilities, his breast glowing with honest pride, conscious that men are born equal, still giving that honour to whom honour is due; he meets at a Great man's table a Squire Something or a Sir Somebody; he knows his noble host at heart gives the Bard or whoever he is a share of his good wishes beyond any at table perhaps, yet how it will mortify him to see a fellow whose abilities would scarcely have made an *eightpenny tailor* and whose heart is not worth three farthings, meet with attention and notice that are forgot to the son of Genius and poverty. . . .

He had smarted recently under some of this snobbish preference in the home of his patron the Earl of Glencairn and the recollection rankled painfully:

> The noble Glencairn wounded me to the soul here because I dearly esteem, respect and love him. He showed so much attention — engrossing attention — one day to the only blockhead at the table — as there was none but his Lordship, dunderpate and myself — that I was within half a point of throwing down my gage of contemptuous defiance; but he shook my hand and looked so benevolently good at parting — God bless him, though I should never see him more, I shall love him to my dying day. . . .

It was the old jealousy of those better endowed materially than himself that sympathetic Gilbert had once pinpointed in an assessment of his clever brother's early character. In Ayrshire he had won plaudits and fame that elevated him among his rural associates; in Edinburgh he was merely a fleeting phenomenon whose "lowness of birth and education" disqualified him from social equality with his "betters"!

From other sources in the country, Robert received well-meant advice that he be on his guard against letting his Edinburgh triumphs go to his head and when the reverend Doctor Lawrie of Loudoun — who had introduced him to the celebrated Doctor Blacklock in Edinburgh — also sounded a paternal warning, he replied that he "had no great temptation to become intoxicated with the cup of prosperity," adding:

> Novelty may attract the attention of mankind for a while, and to it I owe my present *eclat;* but I see that time not far distant when the popular tide that has borne me to a height of which I am, perhaps, unworthy, shall recede and leave me to descend at my leisure to my former station. The consequence is unavoidable and I am prepared for it.

He was far too polite and far too discreet, perhaps, to inform his socially-connected friend that he was becoming rapidly disenchanted by the posturing of those in high places and by their dedication to the symbols of caste and wealth, but he hastened to assure Lawrie that he had no intention of remaining in Edinburgh once the new edition of his *Poems* was launched, declaring:

> I have often felt the embarrassment of my singular situation. However the meteor-like novelty of my appearance in the world might attract attention, I knew very well that my utmost merit was quite unequal to the task of preserving my reputation once the novelty was over.

He had made up his mind, he told Blair, that "abuse and neglect would not surprise him" and he confessed that he was heartily tired of "dodging at the heels of Greatness." Nauseated by the patronizing, lip service and disdain of those in high places, he longed for a breath of fresh air blowing free in rural Ayrshire.

On the 21st of April — five months after his arrival in Edinburgh and after countless parleying with a tardy publisher Creech (whose clients were mostly men above pecuniary hurry) and Creech's printer Smellie — Robert's second edition came off the press. He realized that his *Dedication to the Noblemen and Gentlemen of the Caledonian Hunt* was somewhat sycophantic but he knew on which side his bread had to be buttered. "The Muse had found me at the plough," he told them. "She bade me sing the loves, the joys, the rural scenes and rural pleasures of my native soil, in my native tongue; I tuned my wild, artless notes as she inspired. She whispered to me to come to this ancient Metropolis of Caledonia and lay my songs under your honoured protection; I now obey her dictates." He did not wish to be misunderstood, however, he declared. He was not "approaching his patrons to thank them for past favours or, with the venal soul of a servile author, to ask them for a continuation of those favours." On the contrary, he was "bred to the plough and was independent," he assured them. He "merely came to claim the common Scottish name with them, his illustrious countrymen; and to tell the world that he gloried in the title." He came to "congratulate his country that the blood of her ancient heroes still ran uncontaminated and that, from the Gentlemen of the Caledonian Hunt — with their courage, knowledge and public spirit — protection, wealth and liberty was to be expected." A flattering Dedication, indeed, they agreed and they were willing to condone its expedient sycophancy considering the source from which it emanated.

Robert disposed of the copyright to the second edition of the *Poems* for the sum of one hundred guineas and now turned his attention to a new and tempting project. He had been recently approached by an enterprising publisher called Johnson who was editing a multi-volume *Scots Musical Museum* embodying Scottish songs and poems. It was a project after Robert's own heart and he agreed with alacrity to supply material for it. He was not ready spiritually to return to Mauchline where his sins were not yet forgiven him and the new project would afford him an excellent excuse for delaying his return on the grounds that he wished to take a leisurely jaunt through historic areas of the country that would furnish themes for his muse. As he explained to Frances Dunlop, he "wished to sit on the fields of Scotland's battles, to wander on the romantic banks of her rivers and to muse by the stately towers and ruins once the abode of her heroes."

Impatient to be off, he persuaded Robert Ainslie, an agreeable young law apprentice he had met in Edinburgh — to obtain three weeks leave from his employer in order to accompany him on a tour of the Border country. Eager to visit relatives in that part of the country, Ainslie set out with Robert on the 6th of May when the weather was at its best and the hedgerows were starred with the tiny white banners of the hawthorn. Unable to attend a scheduled meeting of his old Masonic lodge in Mauchline, Robert despatched a hasty note of apology for his absence and conveyed fraternal sympathy for those who were still in arrears with their membership dues:

> Members and Brethren,
>
> I am truly sorry it is not in my power to be at your quarterly meeting. If I must be absent in body, believe me I shall be present in spirit. I suppose those who owe us monies, by bill or otherwise, will appear — I mean those we summoned. If you please, I wish you would delay prosecuting defaulters till I come home — in the meantime to take a note of those who appear and who do not, of our faulty debtors, will be right in my humble opinion; and those who confess debt and crave days, I think we should spare them. . . .

He had known the bitter gall of poverty himself and his heart ached for his hard-pressed companions.

In the carefree days that followed, Robert and the chatterbox Ainslie jogged on by horseback across the dreary Lammermuir hills towards Dunse, Coldstream, Kelso, Jedburgh, Melrose and Yarrow and when Ainslie was obliged to return to Edinburgh Robert journeyed on alone, crossing the Border to visit Alnwick, Hexham, Newcastle and Carlisle. Returning to Scotland he visited Annan and Dumfries where — the countryside ringing with his fame — he was made an honorary Burgess. His thoughts were now concentrated upon the prospect of a return to farming occupation and he was anxious to inspect a farm known as Ellisland, six miles from Dumfries, which had been offered to him by Patrick Miller of Edinburgh who had recently purchased the estate of Dalswinton on which it stood. Unimpressed by the farm — its soil looked stoney and impoverished — he pressed on to Sanquhar and, drawn by an irresistible urge, he turned the head of his pony in the direction of Mauchline. He arrived unexpected and unheralded at Mossgiel and, overcome with emotion, his mother collapsed in his arms crying, "Oh Robert!" He had left Mauchline not many months before miserably poor, in disgrace — hiding from his creditors and shunned by the Armours and their friends, even by Jean herself. Now he had returned with honour and acclaim and with more money in his pockets than he had ever dreamed of possessing.

Limited accommodation at Mossgiel was severely taxed and rather than inconvenience the family and secretly wishing to be free of hampering commitments, he put up at the Whitefoord Arms in the village and, refreshing himself after a hard day's ride, he sat in the gloaming and gave rein to bitter-sweet memories of the days when Jean was at his side. Almost a year had passed since he had crossed the inhospitable threshold of the Armour residence nearby and he longed to flaunt his shining laurels in the face of his former adversaries. He longed passionately to see Jean again, to hold her in his arms and to ascertain the health and well-being of his tiny children. And he wanted to hear from Jean's own lips that the tormenting rumours of her intimate association with Wilson in Paisley had been groundless.

News travelled fast in Mauchline Town and two days later he encountered Jean sunning one of her babes in the courtyard adjoining the Whitefoord Arms. His heart contracted painfully when he observed that she had abandoned the hair ribands that denoted her single status and that she now wore the matron's mutch though there was no ring on her finger. Whatever had happened to them in the past, the present moment was overwhelming to them both, and linking their arms together as though nothing had ever transpired to part them, they slipped into the inn to celebrate their reunion and later Jean went across to her parents' home to beg their permission to bring Robert over to see them. Flesh of her flesh and of his, the tiny child in her arms was an eloquent advocate and their permission was tardily granted and as Robert and Jean, the child now in his arms, crossed the threshold a shaft of golden sunshine made a pathway for their feet. Busy at the ingle when they entered the house, Mary Armour sniffed audibly as they approached but a furtive tear coursed down her averted cheek and James Armour extended a pinch of snuff to Robert to relieve the oppressive tension.

In spite of his happiness in reunion with a now compliant Jean, Robert found it difficult to erase from his mind a recollection of the slights and insults that had once been heaped upon him and he wrote Willie Nicol, an Edinburgh schoolmaster friend: "I never, my Friend, thought mankind capable of anything very generous, but the stateliness of the patricians in Edinburgh and the servility of my plebeian brethren (who formerly eyed me askance) since I returned home have put me out of conceit altogether with my species . . ." and to Frances Dunlop he related, with tongue in cheek, that he had "now been made very welcome to visit his girl." And Frances Dunlop, genuinely fond of Robert, prayed that the course of true love would now run smooth.

CHAPTER 7

Towards the end of June — three weeks after his triumphant return to Mauchline and a period of blissful renewed intimacy with Jean that her parents appeared now to condone — Robert set out alone on a tour of West Argyll, stopping off at Glasgow where he purchased some silk for gowns for his mother and young sisters. He was exceedingly restless, in no mood to settle down and was seriously concerned about his future prospects. In Edinburgh he had enjoyed a taste of personal freedom from hampering commitments that accorded well with his restless and independent spirit and, his physical hungers assuaged for the present by re-possession of Jean, he was in no mood to contemplate matrimonial ties. With many matters to be realistically reviewed, a solo jaunt through the west country would enable him to think more clearly. "I cannot settle my mind," he wrote James Smith who had now gone to Linlithgow to engage in the calico-printing business then coming into vogue. "The only thing of which I know anything — and Heaven knows but little do I understand of that — I cannot, dare not risk on farms as they are. If I do not fix, I will go for Jamaica. Should I stay in an unsettled state at home, I would only dissipate my little fortune and ruin what I intend shall compensate my little ones for the stigma I have brought on their names." Among the "little ones" was now another illegitimate child born to an Edinburgh servant girl he had seen frequently during his stay in that city. He had been privately informed of her plight by an Edinburgh inn-keeper and while, for certain mathematical reasons, he was uncertain of his own blame in the matter, he was willing to do what he could for the unfortunate girl and wrote Ainslie in Edinburgh:

> Please call at the Jas. Hogg mentioned and send for the wench and give her ten or twelve shillings, but don't for Heaven's sake meddle with her as a Piece. I insist on this, on your honour; and advise her out to some country place. You may perhaps not like the business but I must tax your friendship thus far. Call immediately or at least as soon as it is dark, for God's sake, lest the poor soul be starving. . . .

Much as he still loved Jean and much as her once-hostile parents now seemed to regard him with a more indulgent eye, he felt that his first duty lay with the struggling family at Mossgiel. If he failed to locate a suitable farm, emigration to the West Indies for a time would enable him to save a little money for future contingencies that must inevitably be faced. Resumption of conjugal relations with Jean was hazardous and had complicated his legal situation perilously. It rendered the bachelor's certificate in his pocket of dubious value since he had now established a continuing relationship with Jean "by habit and repute." And it made him vulnerable to declaration by the Armours that the original "marriage" was legal when relations were continued. Their plans for marrying Jean off to Robert Wilson in Paisley had misfired, and, believing Robert was now in a position to financially maintain her, they wished for an end to a thoroughly tiresome situation — and for very obvious reasons.

Returning from his West Argyll excursion — and some wondered whether he had been motivated by a sentimental urge to visit Mary Campbell's grave at Dunoon on the Clyde — he spent a few more weeks in Mauchline and, suddenly, on the 8th of August returned to Edinburgh to prod his tardy publisher in the matter of financial settlement.

Johnson was pressing him for more contributions to the *Musical Museum* and, once again, he set out for the Highlands in the company of Willie Nicol, a teacher at the Edinburgh High School, travelling this time by comfortable coach. In search of fresh inspiration for his muse, he visited Linlithgow where Mary Queen of Scots had once been imprisoned; Bannockburn, scene of a famous battle; Cawdor where Duncan had been stabbed to death and Forres where, on "a blasted heath," Shakespeare's Macbeth had met the witches. Learning en route that the tune *Hey, tuttie tatie* had been the battle march of Robert Bruce, he composed some verses embodying an imagined "Address of Bruce to his Army at Bannockburn" with a rousing first line *"Scots, wha hae wi' Wallace bled,"* and married it to the tune for Johnson's *Collection*.

Returning to Edinburgh in high spirits, but still unwilling to make settled plans, he set out early in October on another jaunt, this time in the company of young James Adair, son of an Ayr doctor who was related to Frances Dunlop. Together they visited Stirling and, hospitably entertained en route, they called upon the elderly Mrs. Bruce of Clackmannan Tower who proudly claimed relationship with a descendant of the famous Bruce and laughingly "knighted" Robert, claiming that she had a vested right to do so. At Dunfermline they visited its crumbling abbey where lively Adair mounted the Stool of Repentance as a supposed fornicator and Robert delivered a rebuke upon him similar to the one he himself had once received in Mauchline.

They arrived back in Edinburgh on the 20th of October where Robert found awaiting him the dismaying news that one of Jean's twins — the little girl — had died and that Jean was prostrated with grief. "I hear I am a girl out of pocket and by careless, murdering mischance, too, which has provoked me a good deal," he wrote a Mauchline friend. "I beg you will write me by post immediately on receipt of this and let me know the news of Armour's family and if the world begin to talk of Jean's appearance in any way." Once again, Jean was pregnant.

During his last absence from the city, John Richmond had rented his accommodation to a less restless, more permanent lodger so Robert moved to other quarters in the home of a High School teacher named Cruikshank in a somewhat better district and, early in December, he became involved in a new romance.

Agnes McLehose was exactly the kind of woman to alert Robert. She had long wished to meet the celebrated Mr. Burns, the lion of the social season, but she did not move in the circles in which he was being lionized. Soon, however, her hopes bore fruit and a meeting over the teacups was arranged by a mutual friend, Miss Nimmo, who had already made the acquaintance of Burns via a personal introduction from friends in Ayrshire.

Agnes McLehose was exactly the same age as Robert — give or take three months — and she wrote pretty poetry. She was not exactly a widow but the next best thing — a fascinating young married woman who had been deserted by her husband. A notoriously unsatisfactory husband — always in trouble of one kind or another — he had been persuaded out of the country by relatives who were tired of the embarrassment of his antics. He had taken himself off to Jamaica where, it appeared, he was consorting with dusky belles and founding a mulatto family.

Agnes's five-year marriage had foundered miserably due, it was said, to her husband's "cruelty" and, after bearing him four children in almost as many years, she had been persuaded to return to the home of her father, a Glasgow surgeon, who had been enraged by her marriage at the age of seventeen to the impecunious young bank clerk. "A mad escapade, if ever there was one" he had stormed. Agnes had been no match for the scheming McLehose who, learning that the "pretty Miss Nancy" was to visit Edinburgh on a certain day, had bought up all the seats in the coach in order to have her to himself during the forty-mile journey to the capital city and, when the lumbering coach finally clattered noisily into Edinburgh, the young couple had declared themselves "engaged."

From the very outset, it appeared, the marriage had proved the fiasco it deserved to be. "Only a short time elapsed," wrote Agnes to an intimate friend, "ere I perceived, with inexpressible regret, that our dispositions, tempers and sentiments were so totally different as to banish all hope of happiness between us." Sensibly, she had decided they should go their own ways — McLehose to the far ends of the earth and Agnes to the home of her father in Glasgow. Within a couple of years, however, surgeon Craig died and Agnes decided to go to Edinburgh and place herself and her small children under the wing of her relative Lord Craig, a legal justice who was willing to augment from his own purse the tiny annuity Agnes had inherited from her father's estate. She obtained modest quarters in General's Entry in the Potterrow and settled down to a circumspect grass widowhood.

Agnes was plump, seductive, frivolous and, by her own confession, somewhat lonely. She was charmingly flirtatious and wore perfumed fischus and an enormous tulle bow in her hair so that she looked like a butterfly poised for flight. She lisped engagingly and — according to a contemporary observer — was "of a somewhat voluptuous style of beauty, of lively and easy manners, of a poetical turn of mind with some wit and not too high a degree of refinement."

Although, when they met, Robert was on the verge of returning to Mauchline — this time perhaps for good — since it was necessary to see what might best be done for Jean (her parents had refused to allow a second accouchment in their home) — Robert was reluctant to turn his back upon a new flirtation and, swept off her feet by his impetuosity, Agnes invited him to take tea with her soon in the Potterrow. The sudden illness of her small son William intervened, however, and she was obliged to set another date. "I had set no small store on my tea-drinking tonight and have not been so often disappointed . . . ," Robert wrote her. "Saturday evening next I shall embrace the opportunity with the greatest pleasure." He intended to leave Edinburgh soon —"probably for a twelvemonth," he told her. He would "ever regret he had so recently made an acquaintance he would ever highly esteem and in which he would ever be warmly interested." And, since he had learned that Mistress McLehose was a poetess, he enclosed a poem of his own for her pleasure — "a mere *bagatelle* or *jeu d'esprit* he hoped would please her." He promised to leave more poems for her, too, at the home of the friendly Miss Nimmo, and "hoped she would find them worthy of house room."

But once again fate intervened and their anticipated tea-drinking had to be postponed — this time because Robert had suffered a painful knee injury when the coach in which he had been riding had been overturned by a tipsy coachman. Helped home to his lodgings, he had penned her a hasty note from his new address — St. James' Place:

> I can say with truth, Madam, that I never met with a person in my life whom I more anxiously wished to meet again than yourself. Tonight I was to have had that very great pleasure — I was intoxicated with the idea; but an unlucky fall from a coach has so bruised one of my knees that I can't stir my leg off the cushion. If I don't see you again I shall be vexed with chagrin. I am sorry I have not met you sooner . . . I cannot bear the idea of leaving Edinburgh without seeing you again.

Full of coquettish concern, Agnes sent him a note of condolence, regretting that social convention prevented her from visiting his quarters alone. "Were I your *sister,* I should call upon you," she declared and, deeply moved by her concern, Robert sent her another note by messenger confiding that he "was strangely taken with her and hoped to cultivate her friendship most earnestly." He promised to write her the following day — "and every day thereafter" concluding mysteriously: "Alas! had we only met in time!" Reading his letter a dozen times Agnes tucked it into her bodice and decided she had better remind him that she was a married woman and that, delicious as his compliments were, it was imprudent of him to declare himself so openly. "Pay my addresses to a married woman?" cried Robert in mock concern. "I started as if I had seen the ghost of him I had injured!" Perhaps he *had* "gone a little astray," he conceded, but, after all, who could blame him? Had he not met "an unfortunate woman, amiable, young; deserted and widowed by a man who was bound by every tie of duty, nature and gratitude to protect, comfort and cherish her?" He was full of contrition, he assured her. "Could he say more?" And Agnes conceded happily that, indeed, he could not and decided to let things take an exciting course. She wrote informing him she would be leaving town for a few days to take her ailing child to the seaside for the fresh air he needed and, in reply, Robert begged her to let him know how long she intended to be absent. "I shall count the hours till you inform me of your return," he opined. "Cursed etiquette forbids your seeing me just now and as soon as I can walk again (alas!) I must bid adieu to Edinburgh." Why, oh why had they not met each other sooner, he lamented — "all last winter; these three months past! What luxury of association I have lost — tho' perhaps it was better for my peace of mind." Back and forth by messenger went their sentimental missives between St. James' Place and the Potterrow — as many as four letters between them in a single day.

They met when Agnes returned to town but the neighbours had begun to gossip about Mr. Burns's evening visits to the grass widow in the Potterrow so Agnes suggested it might be better if he came to her house on foot instead of by sedan-chair to be used only for the return home at an hour when her Argus-eyed neighbours were soundly asleep. And, as their letters to each other were often carried by a strange hand, would it not be better for them to sign them with a *nom de plume?* She would sign her letter "Clarinda" — the name used by a female columnist in a local journal — while he would sign his "Sylvander." Perhaps it would be better, too, she declared, if he were to refrain from using the word "love" in his letters and to this he had responded irritably that, if she boggled at the word "love," she might substitute the word "esteem" or any other "tame Dutch expression" she pleased. How could he be expected to substitute "esteem" for "love," he asked. "Love is like adding cream to strawberries. It not only gives the fruit more elegant richness but has a peculiar deliciousness of its own." Agnes found it difficult to resist such beguiling logic and her defences began to crumble. She was suffering from frequent headaches due to the late hours he imposed upon her, she hinted, and she was uneasy about their ripening relations. Her conscience was troubling her, she inferred, and she had taken herself off to the Reverend Mr. Kemp of the Tolbooth Church for counsel and guidance. Her pastor had viewed the matter ecclesiastically, as was to be expected, and he had given her a mild lecture. She had written Robert insisting that he must check his future ardours. But because she appeared to be making mountains out of molehills, Robert had replied that she alone "should decide where the line of discretion should be drawn" and that he would try to be guided by her wishes.

Anonymous letters began to arrive at Agnes's home. They were highly censorious and, in them, Robert shrewdly suspected the hand of the Reverend Mr. Kemp and his henchmen. "I have not the patience to read the puritanical scrawl," he exploded. "Damned sophistry! The half-inch soul of an unfeeling, cold-blooded, Presbyterian bigot cannot forgive anything above his own dungeon bosom and foggy head! You are only answerable to God in such matters," he told Agnes.

Again she closeted herself in the vestry of the Tolbooth Church where her pastor received her kindly but was still censorious. "I saw that he *felt* for me (for I was in tears)," she told Robert, " but he bewailed that I had given my heart while still in bondage. He wished that I had made it *friendship* only and he talked to me in the style of a tender parent anxious for my happiness." She was "sick of the censure of vulgar minds," she told Robert but begged him once again to "restrain his tumultuous passions" and to "visit her less frequently." Her small, dependent children had to be considered. If ugly rumours of her indiscretions were to reach the ears of her guardian Lord Craig who ruled daily on the sins of others, he might even cut off her small allowance and then where would she and her children be? "Had we not better — or had *I* not better exercise a little self-denial?" she asked Robert but to all these trepidations, these foolish alarms and excursions, he thundered an emphatic "No!"

She suggested he might accompany her to the Tolbooth church some Sunday to hear the impressive oratory of the Reverend Mr. Kemp. Perhaps if she and Robert were seen together in the House of God, the tongues of their critics would be shamed into silence. But Robert would have none of such posturings. The hypocrites of Edinburgh were no worse than those elsewhere, he assured her. "But where will you find a sect that numbers no critics?" she countered. She was daily expecting a visit from one of these pests and she dreaded the prospect of his vulgar prying. She must be strictly on her guard, advised Robert. "Should any of these callers question you as to whether *I* am "the man," I do not think they are entitled to any information. As to their jealousy and spite, I despise them! God forgive that these persecutors should harass your peace; it is more precious to me than my own."

He was confronted with more serious problems of his own. If Agnes McLehose had been "widowed by a man who was bound by every tie of duty, nature and gratitude to protect, comfort and cherish her," what about the comfort and protection he now owed Jean? He had received word from Mauchline that, enraged by her new pregnancy, her parents had "turned her out of doors," though, anticipating their rage, she had in reality taken herself off to temporary shelter in the home of relatives in Ardrossan. It was obviously up to Robert to do something about her situation and he had written his friends the Muirs at Tarbolton Mill, asking them to take Jean in until he was sufficiently recovered from his knee injury and could come down to Mauchline to make other arrangements for her welfare.

Her situation was precarious since unmarried women were prohibited by law from setting up establishments of their own. Under the provisions of an ancient statute then extant to a modified degree, Kirk Sessions were required to keep a weather eye open for such irregularities. In earlier times men and women had not even been allowed to associate with each other after nightfall and those suspected of "coming together in suspicious places" were required to purge themselves on oath before the Kirk Elders whose power was absolute. Under a statute dated 1640, young unmarried females (of whatever station in life) were "forbidden to live privately in houses." They were compelled to "betake themselves to domestic service," otherwise they would be dealt with as harlots and they were debarred from "keeping alehouses or taverns." The statute made their position abundantly plain:

> The Session, considering the manifold harlotries and abuses that fall out in the persons of sundrie young women who remain in private houses, ordains that hereafter no young woman of whatsoever quality under whatsoever pretence shall presume to keep private houses within the town but shall retire themselves to honest service under the pain of the censures of the Kirk. Harlots, leaving their service and freeing from the discipline of the Kirk, were forbidden from being entertained by any honest inhabitant.

and in the eyes of the Church, Jean Armour, still unwed by the kirk and continuing conjugal relations with Burns, was in reality pretty close to the designation of "harlot" within its provisions. Banished by her parents and in no position to enter domestic service in somebody else's home, Robert had no alternative but to find some sort of accommodation for her in the village where she could lie low until after her confinement. He could occupy the same domicile for a time, establishing a continuing "marriage by habit and repute" and this would mitigate, to some extent, Jean's parlous situation.

Back once again in Mauchline, — and after a series of painful and stormy interviews with her parents — he was able to obtain the reluctant consent of Mary Armour to stand by her daughter in her new emergency though the Armours refused his suggestion that they should give Jean house room until it was over. He was, however, able to find accommodation for Jean in the village — an upstairs room in a two-storey house in the Backcauseway close to the doctor's "Shop". The house overlooked the kirkyard and it had few domestic comforts if one excluded a gridiron for cooking suspended over a smoke-blackened hearth. "Jean I found banished like a martyr — forlorn, destitute and friendless; all for the good old cause," he wrote Ainslie. "I have reconciled her to her mother; I have taken a room for her; I have bought her a mahogany bed; I have given her a guinea and I have taken her to my arms . . ."

With full knowledge of Robert's embroilment with Agnes McLehose in Edinburgh, Ainslie had little difficulty in understanding the significance of Robert's final paragraph: "I have been prudent and cautious to a degree and I have sworn her privately and solemnly never to attempt any claim on me as a husband, even though anybody should persuade her she has such a claim, which she has not, neither during my life nor after my death . . ." And Jean had "promised all this like a good girl," he declared. She would make no husbandly claim upon him. Still madly in love with him and now solely dependent upon his aid, she was willing to love him on any terms he cared to name.

In the absence of Robert in Ayrshire, Ainslie was seeing a good deal of the fascinating Clarinda who hungered for Robert's news. Impatient for his return to Edinburgh and fearing that his new responsibilities might wean him away from her permanently, Agnes complained peevishly that she had received only one letter from him since his departure and Ainslie passed her anxiety on to Robert. "Tell her I wrote her from Glasgow, from Kilmarnock, from Mauchline and yesterday from Cumnock as I returned from Dumfries," he begged Ainslie and, to set her mind at rest he found time to pen her a few reassuring lines:

> I, this morning, called on a certain woman. I am disgusted with her; I cannot endure her! I, while my heart smote me for the profanity, tried to compare her with my Clarinda: 'twas setting the expiring glimmer of a farthing taper beside the cloudless glory of the meridian sun. Here was tasteless insipidity, vulgarity of soul and mercenary fawning; there, polished good sense, heaven-born genius and the most generous, the most delicate, the most tender passion. I have done with her and she with me. . . .

Refusing to be easily mollified but uncertain as to how far she could go with him, Agnes returned a blistering letter accusing him of fickleness to which, nettled as never before, he replied:

> Clarinda, I have been so stung with your reproach for unkindness — a sin so unlike me, a sin I detest more than the whole Decalogue — that I could not rest in my grave about it were I to die before I see you.
>
> Was it not blasphemy against your own charms and against my feelings to suppose that a short fortnight could abate my passion? You, my love, may have your cares and anxieties to disturb you but they are the usual affairs of life; your future is fixed and your mind in a settled routine. Could you not, my ever dearest Madam, make a little allowance for a man, after a long absence paying a short visit to a country

full of friends, relatives and early intimates? Cannot you guess, my Clarinda, what thoughts, what cares, what anxious forebodings, hopes and fears must crown the breast of a man when no less than his whole future employment and very existence are at stake?

Yes, of course she understood, she assured him penitently. She was secretly afraid, however, that, back in the arms of his Jean who knew how well to enchain him, she might lose him forever. She was only afraid, she told him, that the many miles between them might "gradually wean his heart away from her" and she "counted all things (Heaven excepted) lost that she might win and *keep* him." She knew about Jean's new pregnancy and told Robert she "wished it soon over" and she sent a present of some little shirts for baby Robert at Mossgiel. But fears of a sudden *volte face* on the part of Robert continued to torment her. Once, irritated by her reserves, he had suggested she sue for the dissolution of her marriage with McLehose but to this — with the Reverend Mr. Kemp at her elbow — she turned a deaf ear, urging him to marry somebody else whose passions matched his own. "Dissolve the ties of which you complain, and what do either of us gain?" she had countered. "Some romantic dream of Utopia; but little or no reality. What have either of us to depend on?" She knew there was no early solution of the relationship she had drifted into with ardent Robert but she could not give him up.

Idling for a few days in Mauchline after making the necessary arrangements for Jean, Robert dropped a line to his old friend Captain Brown with whom he had maintained a desultory correspondence since their earlier association in the seaport town of Irvine. "Jean I found with her cargo very well laid in but unfortunately moored almost at the mercy of wind and tide," he told the nautical skipper. "I have towed her into a convenient harbour where she may lie snug until she unload and I have taken command myself, not ostensibly, but for a time in secret. I am gratified with your kind enquiries after her as, after all, I may say with Othello:

> "Excellent wretch! perdition catch
> my soul, but I do love thee!"

There was need for considerable caution and secrecy about his private affairs since efforts were being made by certain Edinburgh friends to obtain employment for him in the Excise service and employees were required to be above reproach in the matter of their domestic affairs.

Still hoping for the ultimate physical conquest of Agnes McLehose despite her hampering religious scruples, he was unwilling, however, to take any definite steps to re-establish his previous "marriage" with Jean openly since there was always the possibility that, enraged by the consequences of his new relations with Jean, her parents might press for marriage or nothing and in this event his days of dalliance with Clarinda would be over. But a bird in the hand is worth two in the bush. Jean had accorded her favours but, to date, Clarinda still hesitated.

Knowing his pigeon well — they had been partners in the past in "many a merry dint" — Brown was little impressed by Robert's proclaimed concern for Jean. Quite recently he had received a letter from Robert declaring that he was "at the moment ready to hang himself for a young Edinburgh widow who had more wit and wisdom more murderously fatal than the stiletto of the Sicilian *banditti*," concluding "For me, I am just about the same Will o' Wisp being I used to be. About the first and fourth quarters of the moon, I generally set out for the trade winds of wisdom; but about the full moon and change, I am the luckless victim of mad tornadoes which blow me into chaos!" Robert's propensity for dual philandering surprised even the rakish Brown whose own sexual excursions — a lass in every port — were proverbial.

Jean was confined early in March and, once again, Robert's "amorous mortgages had paid double." One of the tiny girl children died ten days later, the other shortly afterwards and they were buried in Mauchline Parish Kirkyard as Armour offspring since, ecclesiastically, they were illegitimate. "Man's inhumanity to man made countless thousands mourn," but Jean was too ill to care that her innocent little children had been committed to the ground as bastards and there had been no time for a christening.

And, shortly afterwards, eager to shake the troubled dust of inhospitable Mauchline off his feet, Robert returned to Edinburgh and the beguilements of Clarinda.

CHAPTER 8

Convinced by now that his novelty among the jaded elite of Edinburgh was soon likely to dim and that his popularity was on the wane, Robert decided to take another look at Patrick Miller's farm in Dumfriesshire and this time he took along with him an experienced farmer whose judgment was to be relied upon. In spite of his own misgivings about Ellisland, John Tennant, his farmer friend, had been somewhat encouraging with a result that on the 18th of March — not long after the death of Jean's second twins — he had signed a long-term lease for the 100 acre steading at a rental of £50 per annum for the first three years and £70 per annum thereafter. The lease was for a total period of seventy-six years, broken down into four nineteen-year periods which allowed termination in the event of difficulties and, willing to aid a promising tenant, Miller had agreed to allow Robert the sum of £300 with which to replace the derelict farm-house, to erect other new buildings, to enclose the open fields and to plant a protective screen of trees between the farmhouse and the banks of the river Nith on which Ellisland stood.

To date, the efforts of his patrons in Edinburgh to find rewarding employment for him had met with little success and many of them had advised him to return to his old avocation of farming for which he seemed best suited. Realizing that farming on the limited capital that would be left after he assisted his brother at Mossgiel might well prove suicidal, he had decided to petition the Earl of Glencairn in the matter of recommending him for Government service:

> I am told that your Lordship's interest will easily procure me an Excise grant from the Commissioners; and your Lordship's patronage and goodness, which have already rescued me from obscurity, wretchedness and exile, embolden me to ask that interest. You have likewise put it in my power to save the little tie of *home* that sheltered an aged mother, two brothers and three sisters from destruction. My brother's farm is but a wretched lease but I think he will probably weather out the remaining seven years of it; and after the assistance I have given

and will give him, to keep the family close together, I shall have rather better than two hundred pounds and instead of seeking what is almost impossible at present — a farm that I can live by with so small a stock — I shall lodge this sum in a banking-house for calls of uncommon distress or necessitous old age. . . .

and he added: "My heart sinks within me at the idea of applying to any other of the Great who have honoured me with their countenance. I am ill-qualified to dog the heels of Greatness with the impertinence of solicitation; and tremble nearly as much at the thought of the cold promise as of cold denial."

We do not know whether or not the young Earl — then a sick man who was to die at the early age of forty — replied to the letter or, if he did so, what was the tenor of his reply. It is possible he might have felt somewhat diffident about pressing the interests of Burns in quarters where the Ayrshireman was then being openly discredited. Moreover, the Board of Excise Commissioners was extremely careful about the personal reputation of the men they employed who, being required to deal with the frailties of others, were required to have none of their own. Reports of Burns's Ayrshire scrapes had filtered by degrees into the city. It was commonly known, for instance, that he had fathered an illegitimate child on his mother's maidservant and had been duly rebuked by the Kirk Session in Mauchline. Then there were the children born to Jean Armour and, in Edinburgh itself, he was being sued by a wench named Meg Cameron. Rumours also prevailed that, during his various visits to Edinburgh, he had paid open court to a comely young grass widow in the Potterrow whose lawful husband was out of the country and also that, having given personal offence to a number of prominent Masons, they had recommended he be "disciplined" for his sins. It is possible that the Earl of Glencairn might have hesitated to crave favours for a reckless and irresponsible *protégé*. Help came, however, from quite another quarter and it came soon. Learning of Robert's desire to obtain employment in the Excise service, "Long Sandy Wood," the friendly doctor who had attended him during his knee accident, had seen to it that his name was placed on the roster of applicants and, on the last day of March, a letter was sent by the Board of Commissioners to their superior officer in Tarbolton instructing that Robert Burns of Mauchline was to receive training forthwith. James Findlay, Excise officer in the area, was requested to ensure that the private and personal affairs of the applicant were put in order; that he had "cleared himself and his quarters for both lodging and diet; and that he had on hand sufficient funds to purchase a horse for his duties." Under existing regulations, applicants must not be more than thirty years of age or have more than two children and, should his illegitimate children be counted, he was perilously close to the margin and secrecy about his private affairs was imperative. The Board of Excise Commissioners made no secret of the fact that they preferred married men and, in the routine instructions that Mr. Burns was to be "cleared for lodging and diet," there may have been a hint that a respectable married status was a practical necessity. Inevitably, Jean might be expected to foal again which might well upset his chances for employment in the Excise unless their affairs were put in order. He had confided these expectations to Clarinda and related that he "had been questioned like a child about his private affairs" by his prospective employers and those who had recommended him and that, as a result, he had "almost given up the Excise idea." Still, necessity was driving him hard and, even though he returned to farming, the possession of an Excise commission in his pocket would be insurance against disaster if a new farming venture failed.

Marriage and a settled domicile of his own now appeared imperative since no farmer could farm without the domestic services of a wife. If it had to be marriage, Jean was the only serious contender for the stakes. Even if Agnes McLehose were able to free herself of her bonds, she would be a conspicuous failure as a hard-working farmer's wife, serving the hired help their noon-day broth, tossing hay in the fields or raking muck in the byre! In any event, visions of her desirability were now beginning to fade. Her alarums and excursions had disenchanted him.

He had learned that all that would be necessary to implement his earlier vows to Jean would be their joint appearance before a Justice of the Peace for registration of their previous "irregular" union in the form of *secundum artem* and the payment of a fine. A petition to Mauchline Kirk Session for ecclesiastical recognition of their continuing marriage would follow writing *finis* to a deplorable chapter of events.

Jean was radiant with happiness when Robert outlined his new plans. The lease for Ellisland had already been signed, he told her, and he expected soon to have an Excise commission in his pocket after six weeks' training. Nobody would ever be able to point a finger of scorn at her again.

Early in April — almost two years from their first fateful meeting on the village bleach-green — Robert and Jean proceeded to a nearby inn where, by special arrangement with Gavin Hamilton, the Laird of Gilmilnscroft, J.P. waited to complete the legal details. James and Mary Armour, invited by Robert to attend as witnesses, sent word that they would be out of town for the day. The only "marriage" they were prepared to accept was the Holy Matrimony of the Church.

During his various preoccupations of late Robert had neglected his correspondence badly. Now, however, there was much to relate. His intimate friends would be happy to learn he had put his house neatly in order though there were still reasons why his marriage could not be shouted from the house-tops. He wrote to his mother's brother, his uncle Samuel, who lived on the coast, ordering "three or four stones of feathers during the fowling season" for the nuptial couch:

> It would be a vain attempt for me to enumerate the various transactions I have been engaged in since I saw you last; but this I know; I engaged in a *smuggling trade* and God knows if ever any poor man experienced better returns — two for one; but as freight and delivery have turned out so dear, I have taken out a licence and am beginning in fair trade. . . .

Uncle Samuel had once been in trouble with the law for smuggling; he would lend a sympathetic ear. He also wrote James Smith: "To let you a little into the secrets of my pericranium, there is, you must know, a certain clean-limbed, handsome, betwitching young hussy of your acquaintance, to whom I have lately and privately given a matrimonial title to my corpus" and he ordered a printed shawl for Jean: " 'Tis my first present to her since I have irrevocably called her mine and I have a whimsical kind of wish to get the first said present from an old and much valued friend of hers and mine."

Inevitably, since he was now a marked man in the shire, news of his marriage was certain to leak out and before long he received some carefully worded enquiries from Frances Dunlop, ever inclined to prod and to pry into the private affairs of her *protégé*. "Your surmise, Madam, is correct. I am indeed a husband," he informed her. She had never met Jean personally though she knew something of Robert's early attachment to her and he brought her up to date on the circumstances that had made him a Benedict:

> When she first found herself "as women wish to be who love their lords" — and as I lov'd her near to distraction; I took some previous steps to a private marriage. Her parents got the hint; and, in detestation of my guilt of being a poor devil, not only forbade me her company and their house, but, on my rumoured West Indian voyage, got a warrant to incarcerate me in jail till I should find security in my about-to-be parental relation. You know my lucky reverse of fortune. On my *eclatant* return to Mauchline I was made very welcome to visit my girl. The usual consequences began to betray her; and as I was at that time laid up a cripple in Edinburgh and she was turned, literally turned out of doors, I wrote a friend to shelter her till my return. . . .

He was "not under the least verbal obligation to her," he insisted, "but her happiness or misery were in my hands and who could trifle with such a deposit?" He expected his marriage to turn out well, he declared. "To the least temptation to jealousy or infidelity I am an equal stranger. My preservation from the first is the most thorough consciousness of her sentiments of honour and her attachment to me; my antidote against the last is my long and deep-rooted attachment to her." And to refresh the memory of Frances Dunlop to whom he had not written for some considerable time, he explained that Jean was "the identical woman who was the mother of twins to me twice in seventeen months." He had no apologies to make for her humble status, he declared. It was every bit as good as his own. "In housewifely matters, in aptness to learn and activity to execute, she is eminently mistress; and, during my absence in Nithsdale (where he was building the new farmhouse) she is regularly apprenticed to my mother and sisters in the dairy and other farm business at Mossgiel." Her personal attractions were endearing:

> The most placid good-nature and sweetness of disposition; a warm heart, gratefully devoted with all its powers to love me; vigorous health and sprightly cheerfulness set off to the best advantage by a more than commonly handsome figure; these, I think in a woman may make a good wife though she should never have read a page but the Scriptures of the Old Testament, nor have danced in a brighter assembly than a penny pay wedding. . . .

Knowing that Frances Dunlop, who had frequently urged upon him the wisdom of making a good marriage now that he was being received in high society, was likely to be disappointed by his choice, he had delayed passing his news on to her, preferring to relay it first to her son in the hope it would be relayed to her in due course. She reacted exactly as he had expected her to do and, claiming the privilege of age and indulgent maternal interest, she did not hesitate to express her views. "You are right that a bachelor state would have ensured me more friends," he concurred, "but from a cause you will easily guess, conscious peace in the enjoyment of my own mind and confidence in approaching my God would seldom have been of their number." He had "attached himself to a very good wife," he assured her and, as for her thoughts that Jean might disappoint him socially, insisted:

> Circumstanced as I am, I could never have got a female partner for life who could have entered into my favourite studies, relished my favourite authors, etc. without probably entailing on me at the same time expensive living, fantastic caprice, perhaps apish affectation with all the other blessed boarding-school acquirements which are sometimes to be found among females of the upper ranks — but almost certainly among the misses of the would-be gentry

and because Frances Dunlop herself was a socialite, he added a polite *pardonnez-moi*. He had had enough of the simpering young females who had frequented the Edinburgh salons and a farmer needed a practical down-to-earth wife who would take the rough with the smooth. He was happy and pleased with his choice he told Margaret Chalmers, an Ayrshire friend he had seen something of in Edinburgh and with whom he had once carried on a mild flirtation cut short by the announcement of her engagement to a well-established, well-heeled banker. "Shortly after my return to Ayrshire, I married my Jean . . . nor have I any cause to repent it," he informed her. "If I have not got polite tittle-tattle, modish manners and fashionable dress, I am not sickened and disgusted with the multiform curse of boarding-school affectation; and I have got the sweetest temper, the soundest constitution and the kindest heart in the country." Perhaps he *had* "made some sacrifices," he told Peggy but he was certain that if she knew all the circumstances that had motivated him, she would privately applaud him.

Agnes McLehose in Edinburgh would have to be told of his surprising *volte face* and he dreaded her reaction. He delayed writing her as long as he could, hoping that Ainslie — who was now visiting her more and more frequently — might convey the startling news to her.

In due course the storm of Clarinda's passionate recriminations broke over his head and he received some blistering letters in which she attacked his honour and integrity. Her letters to him and his to her must have been cautiously destroyed but their tenor may be guessed from one of the letters that survives. Written by Robert a few months later, it carried an emphatic denial that he had been guilty of "villainy" and "perfidious treachery":

> As I am convinced of my own innocence, and though conscious of high imprudence and egregious folly, I can lay my hand on my breast and attest the rectitude of my heart; you will pardon me, Madam, if I do not carry my complaisance so far as humbly to acquiesce in the name of Villain, merely out of compliment to your opinion, much as I esteem your judgment and warmly as I regard your worth. I have already told you — and I again aver it — that at the period of time alluded to, I was not under the smallest moral tie to Mrs. B—; nor did I, nor could I then know, all the powerful circumstances that omnipotent Necessity was busy laying in wait for me. . . .

and, turning on the taps of flattery that had always paid handsome dividends, he reminded her that to him alone belonged the credit of preserving her honour:

> When you call over the scenes that have passed between us, you will survey the conduct of an honest man, struggling successfully with temptations the most powerful that ever beset humanity and preserving untainted honour in situations where the austerest Virtue would have forgiven a fall — situations that I will dare to say, not a single individual of all his kind, even with half his sensibility and passion, could have encountered without ruin; and I leave you to guess, Madam, how such a man is likely to digest an accusation of perfidious treachery. Was I to blame, Madam, in being the distracted victim of charms such as yours? Had I seen the least glimmering of hope that those charms would ever have been mine — or had not iron Necessity — but these are unavailing words. . . .

Unavailing they were, stormed a tearful Clarinda to the sympathetic Ainslie who had recently received another letter from Robert in which he declared that he was "truly pleased with his marriage to Jean," and confessed "and it has given a stability to my mind and resolutions unknown before; and the poor girl has the most sacred enthusiasm of attachment to me and has not a wish but to gratify my every idea of her deportment."

Robert's disclosures had hit poor Agnes at a most unfortunate time. Learning that her estranged husband had become prosperous financially in the West Indies and was therefore in a position to support his wife and children in Scotland, a group of philanthropic surgeons — friends of her late father who had augmented her small annuity to the tune of some £8 per annum — had decided to withhold their bounty; and a group of other benevolent-minded gentlemen who had been moved by her plight and had been contributing another £10 per annum, had decided to follow their example. Moreover, her guardian, Lord Craig, had written to the exiled McLehose declaring he was "resolved to advance no more money out of his own funds on account of his family." Coming at such a time, Robert's unexpected desertion was painful. Only a short time before he had written her ardently: "I long to see you; your image is omnipresent to me . . . a hundred times a day do I picture you before your candle, your book or work laid aside as I get within the room. How happy have I been!" And, even more recently: "Life, my Clarinda, is a weary, barren path; and woe to him or her that ventures on it alone. For me, I have the dearest partner of my soul: Clarinda and I will make our pilgrimage together. Wherever I am, I shall constantly let you know how I go on. Will you open with satisfaction and delight a letter from a man who loves you, who has loved you and who will love you to death, through death and forever?" What was she to make now of these passionate avowals? So much for his much-vaunted fidelity and devotion! Yet, in her heart of hearts her sympathy went out to him and there was consolation in the fact that she had told him over and over again that — whether the absent McLehose was a scoundrel or not — she regarded her marriage vows as inviolable and that because of the circumstances she "owed her poor helpless children a double share of parental love." And she had urged him to marry some other woman who was "equally ardent in love as himself" and had counselled him "not to be precipitate in his choice lest, after marriage, he might repent at leisure," while Robert had replied affirming "the improbability of meeting with such a companion." Nevertheless, his repudiation had greatly shocked her and it had taken joy, excitement and comfort out of her forlorn life.

Towards the end of July, after his relations with Jean had been put in order, Robert petitioned Mauchline Parish Church Kirk Session for ecclesiastical consent to their union. It was the time of year when parish scandals of all kinds were cleared away to allow forgiven penitents to present themselves for annual Communion. The Reverend William Auld — by now heartily sick of Robert's philanderings with the fair sex — requested confirmation of a witness to the recent Justice of the Peace ceremony and Robert communicated with James Smith asking him to supply the necessary evidence:

> I have waited on the Reverend Mr. Auld about my marriage and stated that I was legally fined for an irregular marriage by a Justice of the Peace. He says that if I bring an attestation to this by the two witnesses, there shall be no more litigation about it. As soon as this letter comes to hand, please write that "Such things are" and direct your letter to me at Mauchline.

The willing Smith had obliged promptly and, under date of August 5, 1788, a minute confirming the union of Robert and Jean was entered in the Kirk Session records:

Appeared Robert Burns with Jean Armour, his alleged spouse. They both acknowledge their irregular marriage and their sorrow for that irregularity and, desiring that the Session will take such steps as may seem to them proper, in order to the Solemn Confirmation of the said marriage.

The Session, taking this affair under their consideration, agree that they both be rebuked for this acknowledged irregularity and that they be taken solemnly engaged to adhere faithfully to one another as husband and wife all their days.

In this regard, the Session have a title in law to some fine for behoof of the poor and they agree to refer Mr. Burns to his own generosity.

In view of the fact that he was now considered to be an affluent man, Robert's "own generosity" amounted to a donation of a golden guinea. Mauchline Kirk Session had exacted its customary pound of flesh — poor boxes or no.

Feeling somewhat virtuous now, Robert wrote to several distant friends about his new state. One of the letters went to the Reverend Doctor John Geddes, an Edinburgh Roman Catholic priest he had met occasionally at Lord Monboddo's table and with whom he had engaged in conversations on the subject of morality:

As there was ever one side on which I was habitually to blame, I have secured myself by marriage in the way pointed out by Nature and Nature's God. I realized that, to so helpless a creature as a Poet, a wife and family were encumbrances which prudence would shun; but when the alternative was being habitually at eternal warfare with myself on account of habitual follies — to give them no worse name — I must have been a fool to have hesitated and a madman to have made any other choice. . . .

while to James Johnson to whose *Scots Musical Museum* he was now contributing frequently, he declared that he had been "so enamoured of a certain girl's prolific twin-bearing merit that he had given her a legal title to the best blood in his body — and so farewell Rakery!"

He had gone down to Ellisland farm in the month of June, leaving Jean at Mossgiel learning the domestic arts that were to make her a good farmer's wife. There was much to be done at Ellisland before she could be welcomed to her new home. Her younger brother Adam — a promising young mason — went down with Robert to help him dig a well and the days passed for Robert in a flurry of carting lime for the foundations of the new buildings and superintending the labours of artisan masons and carpenters though he shouldered a major share of the work himself. Occasionally, when the weather was fine and he could spare the time, he rode over to Mauchline to spend a few days with Jean and baby Robert and little Bess, and Jean went part of the way to meet him. He composed a special song in her honour to mark what he termed their "honeymoon":

Of a' the airts the wind can blaw
   I dearly lo'e the west,
For there the bonnie lassie lives,

> The lassie I lo'e best:
> There wild woods grow and rivers row,
>> An' mony a hill between;
> By day and night my fancy's flight
>> Is ever wi' my Jean.
>
> I see her in the dewy flow'rs,
>> I see her sweet and fair:
> I hear her in the tunefu' birds,
>> I hear her charm the air:
> There's not a bonnie flow'r that springs
>> By fountain, shaw or green,
> There's not a bonnie bird that sings
>> But minds me o' my Jean. .

Clarinda and her poutings and palpitations seemed very far away.

On the 14th of October, after weeks of hard toil, Robert sent from Ellisland a note to impatient Jean:

> You must get ready for Nithsdale as fast as possible, my dearest Love, for I have an offer of a house in the very neighbourhood with some furniture in it, all of which I shall have the use of for nothing till my own house be got ready; and I am determined to remove you from Ayrshire immediately, as I am a sufferer by not being on my farm myself (during his visits to Mauchline). We will want a Maid-servant of consequence; if you can hear of any to hire, ask for them. The apples are all sold and gone. I am extremely happy at the idea of your coming to Nithsdale as it will save us from these cruel separations. The house is a large one but we will only occupy a room or two of it.

And, early in December, when the ground was covered with newfallen snow and a filigree of sparkling frost adorned the hedgerows, Robert went over to Mauchline to fetch Jean and settle her in their new home. In accordance with old tradition, they were preceded across its threshold by a young servant lass who bore on her head a bowl of salt atop the family bible Robert had recently ordered from London and a few days later he composed a new song that reflected his content:

> I hae a wife o' my ain —
>> I'll partake wi' naebody;
> I'll tak' cuckold frae none,
>> I'll gie cuckold to naebody.
> I have a penny to spend,
>> There — thanks to naebody;
> I have naething to lend,
>> I'll borrow from naebody.
>
> I'm naebody's lord —
>> I'll be slave to naebody;
> I hae a good broadsword,
>> I'll tak dunts frae naebody.
> I'll be merry and free,
>> I'll be sad for naebody;
> If naebody cares for me
>> I'll care for naebody. .

He sent a copy of the song to James Johnson for the *Musical Museum,* promising others as soon as his farm affairs were in order.

During her stay at Mossgiel Jean had become popular with Robert's mother and young sisters for her sweet nature and willingness were endearing. Agnes, the eldest of the three girls came over to Ellisland to assist with the "downsetting" and the merry laughter of the two girls delighted Robert and another song proclaimed his new happiness:

> Louis, what reck I by thee,
>   Or Geordie on his ocean;
> Bankrupt beggar louns to me —
>   I reign in Jeanie's bosom.
>
> Let her crown my love her law
>   And in her breast enthrone me,
> Kings and nations — all awa' —
>   Thieving vagabonds, I disown thee!

He would change places with nobody — not even King Louis of France or "German Geordie" in England.

Neighbouring farmers, long familiar with the poor prospects at Ellisland, shook their heads in secret. After a downpour of rain, the gravelly soil became a quagmire and not even the most optimistic of them could agree that the farm was a bargain.

Although the first months at Ellisland were strenuous and difficult, the days were full of new interests. Letters, newspapers and journals arrived frequently, linking Robert with distant friends and news of Edinburgh's elite continued to interest him; and visitors, passing through the town of Dumfries, found time to visit him at the farm, bringing intellectual stimulus and the latest gossip. From Edinburgh he ordered a selection of books with which to start a circulating library for the benefit of his farmer friends round about, a project that was warmly encouraged by socialite Robert Riddell whose fine estate, Friar's Carse, adjoined Ellisland and who had bestowed upon Robert a key to his private park where he might find seclusion in which to meditate.

Publishing matters took him once again to Edinburgh but Agnes Mc-Lehose refused to see him, telling Ainslie — who was to pass the news on — that she intended to stay away from her windows in case she caught even a glimpse of him. Her chagrin and humiliation still rankled.

Now settled happily in quite another world, however, he felt little inclination to look her up or to visit his former friends and hosts and he reported to Frances Dunlop after he returned to Ellisland: "Here I am, Madam, returned safe from the capital. To a man who has a home, however humble — if that home is like mine, the scene of domestic comfort — the bustle of Edinburgh will soon be a business of sickening disgust." He detested its "vain pomp and glory" and its "worship of rank and privilege," he told her; and he despised "the insolence of condescension" to which he had once been subjected and the fawning he had seen lavished on the "lobster-coated puppies" of the

Caledonian Hunt Club. And he scorned the "funeral pomp paraded for the carcass of Greatness." He had not forgotten the slights he had suffered at the hands of some of these Edinburgh gentry. A prominent host, seeking entertainment for his jaded guests, had invited him to dine but he had been ushered into the servants' hall to eat and, filled with resentment and anger, he had turned on his heel and left, sending a poem later to his startled host:

> My Lord, I would not fill your chair
> Tho' ye be proudest noble's heir!
> I came this night to join your feast
> An equal of the best at least!
> 'Tis true that cash with me is scant
> And titles trifles that I want:
> The King has never made me kneel
> To stamp my manhood with his seal:
> But what of that? The king on high
> Who took less pains with you than I,
> Has filled my bosom and my mind
> With something better of its kind
> Than your broad acres — something which
> I cannot well translate to speech:
> But by its impulse I can know
> 'Tis deeds, not birth, that makes men low.
> Your rank, my Lord, is but a loan:
> But mine, thank Heav'n, is all my own!
> A peasant — this my pride to be —
> Look round and round your halls and see
> Who boasts a higher pedigree
>
> I was not fit, it seems to dine
> With these fox-hunting heroes fine,
> But only came to bandy jests
> Among your Lordship's hopeful guests.
> There must be here some sad mistake —
> I would not play for such a stake:
> Be a buffoon for drink and meat
> And a Poor Earl's tax paid seat.
> No, die my heart, 'ere such a shame
> Descend on Robert Burns's name!

Busy with constant agrarian interests, the landed gentry of Dumfriesshire were a vastly different breed to the hothouse Edinburgh variety and, if his once-bright laurels were now beginning to fade a bit, he found little diminution in the goodfellowship they extended to him and he was a welcome guest at their tables. He hoped, in the fulness of time, they might accept Jean, too, and he was determined she should appear to advantage sartorially among their wives and daughters. Daily his love for her deepened and he composed another song in her honour:

> O, were I on Parnassus hill
> Or had of Helicon my fill,

That I might catch poetic skill
To sing how dear I love thee;
But Nith must be my Muse's well,
 My Muse must be thy bonnie sel';
On Corsicon I'll gaze and spell
And write how dear I love thee.

Then come, sweet Muse, inspire my lay!
For a' the live-long summer's day
I couldna sing, I couldna say
How much, how dear I love thee.
 By night and day, a-field, at hame
The thoughts o' thee my breast inflame;
And ay I muse and sing thy name,
I only wish to love thee.
Tho' I were doomed to wander on
Beyond the sea, beyond the sun,
Till my last weary sand was run;
Till then — and then — I'd love thee!

Ellisland, with its enchanting vistas of rural beauty in every direction, its silver ribbon of the shining river Nith threading its way among lush pastures, was to be their home for almost three years and here two more sons were born to them. Later on, when new cares, disappointments and failing health began to dog Robert's footsteps, he was to declare that these early days at Ellisland had been the happiest of his life. He could see the golden grain ripening in his fields; the farm creatures he loved so well waited for his coming and, on the verdant banks of the river he was able to ramble at his leisure. He had an Excise commission in his pocket against future financial set-backs and he heard the happy laughter of his children and those he loved at his own fireside. And Jean — who had gone down into the very pit of despair for his sake in the past — was daily at his side inspiring lines that were to become immortal:

To mak' a happy fireside clime
 To weans and wife
That's the true pathos and sublime
 Of human life. . .

For the first time in all his troubled, ill-starred life, the heart of Robert Burns was at rest.

CHAPTER 9

Apart from the spiritual satisfaction he derived from his role of independent farmer, Robert was little enamoured of the social conditions prevailing in his new parish. They seemed little better than those that had irritated him in Tarbolton and Mauchline previously. Writing to John Beugo, an Edinburgh engraver who was working on his portrait for a new edition of the *Poems* and with whom he had once shared French lessons in the capital city, he complained: "I am here at the very elbow of existence in that most pleasurable part of life called social communion. The only things that are to be found here in any degree of perfection are stupidity and canting" and of canting he had had more than enough in his two former parishes. Most of his new neighbours seemed to set little store on the fact that a celebrity had come among them, nor did they appear to appreciate poetic talents *per se*: "Prose they know only in prayers and graces and, as for the Muses, they have as much idea of a rhinoceros as of a poet!" he declared. He missed his old cronies in Mauchline who were willing to pay generous tribute to his talents.

Knowing that he was now settled down at Ellisland, publisher Johnson urged him again for new contributions for a third edition of the *Musical Museum* and during the long winter evenings when the plough was laid aside in the barn, Robert worked over some of the new themes he had gathered previously during his tours of the Border country and the west Highlands. In addition, he was eager, he told Johnson, to try his hand at some love poems — always a favourite theme — and queried him: "Have you never a fair goddess that leads you a wild-goose chase of amorous devotion? Let me know a few of her qualities, such as, whether she be dark or fair; plump or thin; short or tall, etc. and choose your tune and I shall task my Muse to celebrate her." He posted a parcel of new and "refurbished" songs to Johnson every fortnight and still the publisher asked for more. He had pressing problems on his mind, however, and sometimes his enthusiasm for Johnson's venture flagged. He discovered early that the new farm was not the white hope he had been encouraged to expect it to be and, by the middle of September, he decided to apply to Graham of Fintry, senior Excise officer in the area, outlining his difficulties and hinting that he might apply for an Excise position if things did not improve: "I look upon my Excise commission as my sheet anchor in life," he told Graham:

> My farm, now that I have tried it a little, tho' I think it will in time be a saving bargain, yet does by no means promise to be such a penny-worth as I was taught to expect. It is in the last stages of worn-out poverty and will take some time before it pay the rent. I might have had the cash to supply the deficiencies of these hungry years, but I have a younger brother and three sisters on a farm in Ayrshire; and it took all my surplus, over what I thought necessary for my farming capital, to save not only the comfort but the very existence of that fireside family circle from impending destruction. This was done before I took the farm; and rather than abstract my money from my brother, a circumstance that would ruin him, I will resign the farm and enter immediately into the service of your Honours. But I am embarked now in the farm; I have commenced married man; and I am determined to stand by my lease, till resistless necessity compel me to quit my ground. . . .

"Resistless Necessity" was not long in overtaking him, however, and he wrote again to Graham with a tangible suggestion. There was one solution that might enable him to ride out his storms — immediate employment as an Exciseman. He had been told that one of the officers in the area had recently fallen heir to a comfortable legacy and it had been rumoured that he intended to relinquish his position. With a little delicate investigation and subject to the rules of the Service respecting seniority, could not Leonard Smith's position be made available to him? he asked Graham: "The removal of Smith would do him no manner of injury and, on a month's warning to give me a little time to look again over my Instructions, I would not be afraid to enter on business. It would suit me to enter on it at the beginning of next Summer." But, after he had posted the letter, he had conscientious scruples about taking the bread out of another man's mouth should the rumours prove unfounded and he wrote again to Graham offering another suggestion: "I was thinking that, as I am only a little more than five miles from the town of Dumfries, I might officiate there if any of the officers could be removed with more propriety than Mr. Smith . . . I could not bear to injure a poor fellow by ousting him to make way for myself, but to a wealthy son of good fortune like Smith, the injury is imaginary where the propriety of your rules admits." Matters were set in motion by the well-disposed Graham and the petition was granted. His salary was to be £50 per annum for a rural patrol but there were sizeable perquisites in the form of a percentage of the fines collected and Robert wrote to Ainslie in Edinburgh that he had been "very lucky" and that, while he was not too proud of the work he would be called upon to perform — searching for illicit whisky stills and goods smuggled over from France — one had to be realistic when one's very livelihood were at stake. "I have seen the day when my auditory nerves would have felt very delicately on this subject; but a wife and children are things which have a powerful influence in blunting such sensations," he averred. Moreover, the Excise service made provision for the widows and children of deceased officers. Altogether, "this is no bad settlement for a Poet," he told Ainslie.

He also relayed the news of his appointment to Lady Glencairn, mother of his Edinburgh patron the Earl. Sending him copies of some of her own poems, she had wished him well. "People may talk as they please about the ignominy of the Excise," he declared, "but £50 a year will support my wife and children and keep me independent of the world; and I would much rather have it said that my profession borrowed credit from me, than that I borrowed from my profession." For all his rejoicing, however, the stool-pigeon work he would be called upon to perform weighed heavily on his heart and conscience and he composed some lines that reflected his feelings:

> Searching auld wives' barrels,
> Och — hon! the day!
> That dirty yeast should stain my laurels:
> But — what'll ye say?
> These movin' things ca'd wives and weans
> Wad move the very heart o' stanes!

Robert's personal correspondence increased greatly after his settlement at Ellisland for, disappointed by his reception in Dumfriesshire, he longed to keep in touch with his old Ayrshire friends. Of late he had received a few letters from his youngest brother William who, after a futile search for employment as a saddler in his own country, had crossed the border into England where he had obtained temporary work in Newcastle-on-Tyne. William was a mildly pricking thorn in Robert's flesh. He was timid and irresolute and lacked the initiative Robert had tried constantly to engender in him exhorting him to "build resolution and play the man." He had been unable to devote much time to William's problems (having many of his own) but he had tried to find him employment and he had told him that, should he ever run seriously short of money, he could always find a bed and a bite at Ellisland. William, it now appeared, was involved in his first love affair. He had asked his experienced elder brother for advice and Robert had replied kindly:

> Your falling in love is indeed a phenomenon. To a fellow like yourself it cannot be hurtful. I am, as you know, an old veteran in these campaigns, so let me advise you always to pay your particular attentions and try for intimacy as soon as you feel the first symptoms of the passion; this is not only best but it is a preservative for one's peace. I need not caution you against guilty amours — they are bad and ruinous everywhere, but in England they are the very devil. . . .

and with vivid recollections of the seamy side of life in Edinburgh still fresh in his mind, he cautioned William against prostitutes and the ruin they brought in their train. Similar advice had once been expressed in his poetic *Epistle* to young Andrew Aiken, son of lawyer Aiken to whom he had dedicated his poem *The Cotter's Saturday Night:*

> The sacred lowe o' well-plac'd love
> Luxuriously indulge it;
> But never tempt th' illicit rove,
> Tho' naething should divulge it;
> I wave the quantum of the sin,
> The hazard o' concealing;
> But Och! it hardens a' within,
> And petrifies the feeling!

It was a long Epistle concluding:

> Adieu, dear, amiable Youth!
> Your heart can ne'er be wanting;
> May prudence, fortitude and truth
> Erect your brow undaunting!
> In ploughman phrase, "God send you speed,"
> Still daily to grow wiser;
> And may ye better reck the rede
> Than ever did th' Adviser

We do not know whether or not brother William profited by his advice but some months later, after he had moved on to London in search of more permanent employment, he succumbed to an epidemic then raging in the city and John Murdoch, their boyhood tutor, attended the funeral as chief mourner and Robert paid poor William's funeral expenses.

From Ellisland, Robert carried out his new Excise duties conscientiously and competently and his superiors were well pleased by his resourcefulness when he suggested additional avenues of collectible revenue that had been previously overlooked. But Jean was becoming increasingly worried that the new duties superimposed on the work of the farm might soon overtax his strength. He was obliged, in all weathers — rain or shine — to ride two hundred miles a week in "rides" covering ten far-flung parishes and he worked far into the night compiling account books and records.

In the month of August, not long before he had commenced his Excise duties, Jean had borne another son, named Francis Wallace in honour of Robert's old friend Frances Dunlop and he had written her: "I cannot help congratulating you on his looks and spirits. Every person who sees him acknowledges him to be the finest, handsomest child he has ever seen. I am, myself, delighted with the manly swell of his little chest and a certain miniature dignity in the carriage of his head and the glance of his fine black eye, which promise the undaunted gallantry of an independent mind." He hoped for a large family, he told her, but wished that "Heaven would be so obliging as to let him have a family in a proportion of three boys to one girl." He hoped to "show a set of boys that would honour his name," he declared. He did not feel equal to rearing girls, he opined, "Besides, I am too poor and

84

a girl should always have a fortune." If Jean, for instance, had had money of her own, how different things might have been for them.

As the months wore on, however, and they entered another unpromising year, his letters to intimate friends began to reflect more than pride in his growing family. They mirrored a flagging enthusiasm for farming on limited capital. Once he had believed, he told them, that farming was the best possible life for a man but when a farmer "had to pay a dear, unconscionable rent it was a cursed life," he complained. It was a very different matter for the man who farmed his very own acres — "sowing his own corn in hope and reaping it in gladness; shearing his own flocks, rejoicing at Christmas and begetting sons and daughters until he became the venerated gray-haired leader of a little tribe." Why, *then,* he declared, it was "a Heavenlife! But devil take the life of reaping the fruits another man must eat!" From his earliest years — previously at the farms of Mount Oliphant and Lochlie when his father was alive and later at Mossgiel — he had had more than a nodding acquaintance with poverty and the grim spectre of the harrassing rent collector he had depicted in *The Twa Dogs.* Now the pattern was being repeated at Ellisland. "I am jaded to death with fatigue," he told Nicol in Edinburgh and to sympathetic Gilbert at Mossgiel he complained: "My nerves are in a bad state. I feel that horrid hypochondria pervading every atom of my body and soul. But let it go to hell! I'll fight it out and then be off with it. If once I was clear of this damned farm I could rest more easily." And Gilbert recalled all too vividly how poor Robert, when young, had been obliged to plunge into a tub of cold water kept at his bedside, for alleviation of the rheumatic pains and heart palpitations that were a legacy of unremitting toil at a too-early age. It was at Mount Oliphant and Lochlie that the seeds were sown for the acute endocarditis that would one day kill his brother.

During the early days at Ellisland Jean shouldered a major share of the farm work as best she could in the infrequent intervals of child-bearing. They were assisted by two male labourers and two women on the domestic front who had been recruited in Ayrshire. There were nine or ten milch cows to look after; four horses for ploughing and transportation and several pet sheep Robert was greatly attached to. The animals had to be fed and watered regularly and there were hot mashes to prepare for them when the ground was white with snow.

From time to time letters arrived from Frances Dunlop to relieve Robert's gloom but her excessive maternalism, her constant advice, sometimes irritated him. She had heard rumours about his failing health and suggested that, using his horse so much, he might be depriving himself of healthful exercise and he had replied that he "got plenty of exercise" but that part of his malaise was due to the amount of liquor he was obliged to consume at the tables of his friends. "Occasionally hard drink is the devil to me," he confessed, "and against this I have again and again bent my resolution and I have greatly succeeded. Taverns I have totally abandoned but it is the private parties in the family way among the hard-drinking gentlemen of the country that do me the mischief," he told her.

With good-natured tolerance and patience Jean succeeded now and then in coaxing him out of his black moods — his "blue devil hours" he liked to call them. Sometimes he was short with the servants and flew into rages about their shortcomings. Once, taking the easy way out in cutting up potatoes for the cattle, a servant had caused grief. The large lumps had gagged them and, enraged by her stupidity, Robert raged and ranted though his anger was usually short-lived and he was penitent afterwards. Occasionally he became restless and strained at the connubial harness. Not that he loved Jean less but Nature had never intended him to be caged and he chafed at his bonds. Deaf to malicious reports that he consorted with lavish barmaids on his "rides" about the countryside, Jean went serenely on her way, refusing to complain or restrain him. She was "a good and prudent housewife, kept everything neat and tidy and was popular with the servants for whom she provided plenty of wholesome food," reported her neighbours. Mr. Burns might not be the ideal farmer, they agreed, but Jean was an ideal farmer's wife. She was a devoted mother to her bairns and always commendably cheerful. Anxious that she should appear to advantage in the homes he now visited, Robert encouraged her to dress neatly and he coached her in social deportment, but she was seldom invited to their tables and she was far too philosophical and much too busy with her children to care. She had been long accustomed to social ostracism and she had never learned that, meeting her for the first time, one of her husband's snobbish patrons had declared that, in eulogizing her charms, Mr. Burns had "used his imagination!" As far as she was concerned, Robert was the star turn and she was happily content to retire into the background.

Added to his routine duties on the farm, his Excise work allowed him scant time for poetizing but a chance introduction by Robert Riddell to a genial Captain Grose — a well-known antiquary who was compiling a two-volume work on Scotland's historic landmarks — spurred him to new efforts. The agreeable Grose, whose enormous girth made him the butt of good-natured mirth, was staying with the Riddells at Friar's Carse and as Robert's enthusiasm for the songs and legends of his native country ran parallel to Grose's own, the two men spent stimulating hours together whenever Robert was free. Recalling the old ruined kirk at Alloway and the kirkyard in which his father had been buried, Robert suggested to Grose that he include a picture of the storied landmark in his work and, readily consenting, Grose had invited Robert to compose a poem to accompany the picture. Superstitious peasants in the area had long held the old kirk was haunted and that it was the scene of wild revels held by witches at the dark of the moon. Robert's imagination rioted and, recalling a disreputable old farmer who lived on a farm called Shanter nearby, he posed the tipsy "Tam" in a spirited saga and titled it *Tam o' Shanter*. The poem was the work of a single night as he wandered along the banks of the river Nith in the gloaming. Jean, who had wandered out to join him there, had been halted in her tracks by his excited gestures as he recited it to himself and, rather than disturb him, she had returned to the house alone. Reading the poem in full to her later on, he declared it the best poem he had ever written — a verdict in which Frances Dunlop concurred when she received a copy of the volume containing it. She had been "transported" by the vision of an inebriated "Tam" who, disturbing the witches at their revels, had been obliged to ride his old mare Maggie post-haste for an old stone bridge where he would be safe from their rage since witches had no power over running water!:

> And scarcely had he Maggie rallied,
> When out the hellish legion sallied.
> As bees buzz out wi' angry fyke,
> When plundering herds assail their byke,
> So Maggie runs, the witches follow
> Wi' mony an eldritch skreech an' hollow. . . .

The witches "flew at Tam wi' furious ettle but little wist they Maggie's mettle:"

> One spring brought off her master hale,
> But left behind her old gray tail;
> The carlin caught her in the rump
> An' left poor Maggie scarce a stump. . . .

His poetic aspirations re-kindling under spiritual content at Ellisland, he had composed a poignant poem to mark the anniversary of Mary Campbell's death in the month of October and he read it to Jean at the end of a hard day's work. He had confidence in her critical judgment, he once told a friend, declaring that he was "not ashamed to admit that he had often profited by it."

When the long winter nights set in, he turned once more to long-neglected correspondence with distant friends, bringing them up to date on his family news. "I have two fine, healthy, stout little fellows and I have a thousand reveries and schemes about them and their future destiny," he related. He had decided "never to breed up a son of his to any of the learned professions," he declared. "I know the value of independence and since I cannot give them an independent fortune, I shall give them an independent way of life." He still believed, deep in his heart, that "independence at the plough-tail" was the best life for a man and he hoped his sons would follow in his footsteps.

By the end of the third year at Ellisland, however, it was clearly apparent that its grudging and unresponsive acres could never be coaxed into providing a family living and as his landlord, Patrick Miller, had received an offer for the farm from a farmer whose lands adjoined Ellisland, Robert decided to relinquish his lease since he had now been promoted to the Port Division of the Excise, located in the town of Dumfries some five miles away. His new salary would be £70 per annum and he would no longer be required to maintain a horse in a "foot-walk."

Thankful to ease out of the nightmare of Ellisland, Robert lost little time in making arrangements for the disposal of his crops and farm implements and the transfer of his family to new quarters in the lively market town of Dumfries. His crops sold well, the bidders constantly plied with liquor to subsidize their enthusiasm. "I sold my crop recently and sold it well," he wrote a friend in England, "A guinea an acre, on an average, above value. But such a scene of drunkenness was hardly ever seen in this country. After the roup was over, about thirty people engaged in a battle, every man for his own hand, and fought it out for three hours. Nor was the scene much better in the house. No fighting, indeed, but folks lying drunk on the floor and decanting, until both my dogs got so drunk by attending them that they could not stand. You will easily guess how I enjoyed the scene: as I was no farther over than you used to see me."

Heartbroken by the turn of events, Jean viewed the impending move to Dumfries with dismay. It was true that, with Robert's improved salary and no strenuous physical work, they might be better off in the long run but, accustomed to the freedoms of Ellisland and a comparatively spacious farmhouse, it would be difficult for them to adjust to a new kind of life in cramped quarters. They would be exchanging a new dwelling made cosy by her own domestic arts, for three wretched little rooms and a tiny kitchen on the second floor of a dismal-looking house in a depressing district of Dumfries known as the Stinking Vennel due to its proximity to the quay where receding tides left a tangle of nauseous effluent. Instead of enchanting vistas of the River Nith, lush pastures and fields of golden grain and hedgerows starred with blossom, there would be nothing to meet the eye but dingy cobblestones, ugly roof-tops and smoke-belching chimney-pots. At Ellisland Jean had been the proud mistress of a sizeable establishment of children, hired help and frequent visitors. At Ellisland, pretty young Fanny Burns, daughter of Robert's impoverished uncle Robert, had found romance with Jean's younger brother Adam, soon to be apprenticed to mason Armour in Mauchline and her favorite sister Helen (Nellie) had often stayed with them in the early days at the new farm and so had Robert's friendly young sister Agnes. A young Burns cousin had helped out during the harvest season and when baby Francis was born — their first child in holy wedlock — Robert's mother had come to lend a helping hand. In keeping with their status as master and mistress at Ellisland, Robert and Jean had taken their meals in the privacy of a carpeted parlour where there was room for Robert's treasured desk and bookcase which would now have to be squeezed into a tiny alcove in the rooms in Dumfries.

At Ellisland Jean had dressed neatly, even elegantly to please Robert. She wore silk stockings, kid gloves (a luxury sometimes smuggled over from France), a brooch set with pebbles, a pair of gold ear-rings and a variety of

88

becoming shawls. In Dumfries she would join the ranks of the humblest female townsfolk and fishwives, shaking dusty mats out of a second-floor window and slinking down dingy alleys after it was dark to get a reviving breath of fresh air. She knew all too well what it meant to live in cramped quarters in a seedy district. The memory of the room she had shared with Robert in Mauchline's Backcauseway came back to her now and the prospective move to Dumfries filled her with anguish. For poor, tired Robert's sake, she resolved to face the future courageously, however, and she was cheered by the thought that, in Dumfries, there might be better educational opportunities for their small sons in the years that lay ahead. Recriminations were futile now, she knew, but tormenting thoughts often assailed her. If only Robert had applied himself a little more industriously to the work of the farm instead of leaving it sometimes to irresponsible hired help that took full advantage of his absence. If only he had not devoted himself so whole-heartedly to the composition of poems and songs for which he refused to accept a penny from publishers. If only he had not squandered quite so much time organizing the Monkland Friendly Society and a circulating library for the benefit of his neighbours. And if only he had been able to ignore for a time the avalanche of letters that had descended upon him daily from Ayrshire, Edinburgh, Glasgow, London and points further afield, leaving him often still at his desk when dawn broke over the mist-wreathed fields. It was no use repining now however. The die was cast; the crops were sold and Ellisland was being dismantled. She packed her belongings in silence and went out to the byre and barn to bid a sentimental farewell to the beasts that had served them so well. It was torture to see them driven off to the slaughter-house. The only animal Robert had agreed to spare was the pretty little heifer that had been a belated wedding gift from Colonel Dunlop, son of his kind patron at the Dower House.

On a chilly November morning when the fields glistened with the first hoar-frost of the season and the skies were heavy with unshed snow, they set out for the town of Dumfries. Robert rode ahead on the horse he had decided to keep for a while and Jean and the children followed closely behind on a cart containing their household gear — a bare minimum of possessions that could be reasonably accommodated in the tiny rooms in Dumfries; and the little brown heifer trotted sedately in the rear. As they rode past long-familiar landmarks pregnant with memories of the past three years, Jean brushed away a scalding tear. She dared not look back at the fast-receding chimneys of Ellisland. Part of her heart and all of her dreams of the kind of life she loved passionately lay buried there.

CHAPTER 10

For his part, Robert entertained no such misgivings and indulged in none of these introspections. He regarded the abandonment of Ellisland and his last fling at farming more philosophically. It was true that the disastrous venture on too little capital had divested him of most of the profits he had received from the Edinburgh edition of his *Poems* and that the loan of £180 to Gilbert at Mossgiel had been made at considerable sacrifice to the family; but the years at Ellisland had satisfied once and for all his spiritual yearning for the type of life that had nourished his forebears.

It was painful for him to reflect that, in the eye of his traducers — among them the half-won-over Armours — he would be rated a failure — he who had so often in the past exposed the shortcomings of the Holy Willies and the Unco Guid. But life in Dumfries would be full of new challenges and distractions and, with even more miles between them, the Armours were not likely to darken his doorstep often. Dumfries — "Queen of the South" — with its population of approximately six thousand inhabitants offered fine opportunities for social and cultural pursuits. From time to time, members of the Dumfriesshire and Galloway Sporting Club descended upon the town for an orgy of sporting events by day and cards, gambling and dancing by night; and once a year members of the elite Caledonian Hunt arrived to participate in the contest for the silver James VI gun which was awarded on the King's Birthday: and, following in their wake, came the families of the contestants, their carriages, valets and wig-makers and the taverns and hostelries of the town bulged to capacity. Best of all, to Robert's way of thinking, was the fact that Dumfries and its neighbourhood provided a ripe field for the exercise of his Muse. It was rich in stirring historical lore of clan warfare and border raids that had enriched the history books.

After contributing numerous songs and verses to Johnsons' *Musical Museum,* he had found himself deeply committed to enrich the five-volume publishing venture of Thomson along similar lines. He had been requested to contribute "twenty or twenty-five songs suited to particular melodies" for Thomson's *Select Collection of Original Scottish Airs for the Voice*. The work was to be launched as *Symphonies and Accompaniments for the Pianoforte and Violin with Select and Characteristic Verses by the Most Admired Scottish Poets* and Thomson had recruited the services of such famous musicians as Pleyel and Kozeluch for the melodies. Mr. Burns was to provide original verses of his own and to tone down for polite ears some of the popular bawdy ballads then in circulation. Thomson declared he "was willing to pay him any reasonable price he should be pleased to demand" and that profit from the project would be "quite a secondary consideration." And Robert, so enthused by the proposition that he was unable to concede, even to himself, that publishers rarely published for altruistic reasons, had promptly replied: "As to any remuneration, you may think my songs either *above* or *below* price; for they shall be absolutely one or the other. In the honest enthusiasm with which I embark in your undertaking, to talk of money, wages, fee, hire, etc. would be downright sodomy of soul!"

This sort of talk infuriated Jean for, without the farm produce to fall back upon for provisions, they would be hard pressed to make ends meet in Dumfries even though Robert's new salary would be slightly better, and she saw no reason why he should not be amply rewarded for his time and talents. But she kept these rebellious feelings to herself and encouraged him to plunge himself whole-heartedly into Thomson's project and for the next five years — while Mozart was composing *The Magic Flute* and Boswell was writing his important *Life of Samuel Johnson,* he laboured cheerfully for the two publishers though his Excise duties compelled him to work from five o'clock in the morning until seven at night and sometimes longer. How long he would be able to burn the candle at both ends seemed problematical to a worried Jean.

The change of residence from Nithsdale to Dumfries, with all the inconveniences of the new life in the latter, was not the only change she found hard to cope with. Overtaxing his physical strength atrociously at Ellisland, he had developed a nervous irascibility that prostrated him and was accentuated under such minor afflictions as a bout of influenza, a siege of toothache or a fall from his horse. His temper was sparked, like a paper bonfire, by such trivial things as the lusty cries of the children clamouring for food and attention, the arrival of a tradesman's overdue bill or new evidence of the jealousy or ill-will of unsympathetic enemies. Illogically enough, it seemed, he was even resentful of Jean's amazing fertility. "Mrs. Burns seems determined to make me the patriarchal leader of a band," he wrote Frances Dunlop and to another correspondent he declared — doubtless with tongue in cheek — that he "rejoiced at Jean's remarkable twin-bearing abilities." Not yet twenty-five she had already borne him two sets of twins and two more sons and another child was expected. She was a born matriarch, he knew. She had taken a warm maternal interest in the well-being of his child by Lizzie Paton and when, during one of her infrequent visits to

Mauchline, he had inadvertently fallen into the arms of a barmaid at the Globe Inn in Dumfries, she had gathered that child, too, into her arms and had placed it in the cradle prepared for her own child born ten days later, remarking laughingly to a friend "Our Robert could hae done with *twa* wives!" And when James Armour, dropping in on them a little later on to see his newest grandchild, had enquired incredulously whether she had again born twins, she had told him that Ann Park's child was the bairn of a neighbour she was looking after during its mother's temporary absence. With loving tolerance and good-natured generosity, she had ignored Robert's latest "slip," knowing all too well that poor Robert in his cups was likely to commit transgressions he would never have done in the cold light of rational sobriety. He was invariably lonely and depressed during her absences and Ann Park, niece of the hostess of the Globe Inn, was a comely and flirtatious wench whose favours were easily come by. Always contrite after such lapses, he had once told an intimate friend that "a wife's head was immaterial to her heart" in such matters:

> The scale of good wifeship I divide into ten parts: good nature, four; good sense, two; wit, one; personal charms, i.e. a sweet face, eloquent eyes, fine limbs, graceful carriage — all these things, one. As for the other qualifications such as Fortune, Connections, Education, Family Blood, etc., divide the remaining two degrees among them as you please. . . .

Susceptible as he was to female physical charms, he was willing to place good nature at the top of the list and waxed lyrical about Jean's attractive endowments:

> As fine a figure and face as could be produced in any station and rank of life whatever; rustic, native grace; unaffected modesty and unsullied purity and a simplicity of soul; Nature's mother wit and — the dearest charm of all the rest: a yielding sweetness of disposition and a generous warmth of heart, grateful for love on my part and ardently glowing with more than equal return. . . .

Contemplating another visit to Edinburgh in connection with recovery of funds from publisher Creech, Robert thought often of the recently-abandoned Clarinda and wondered how she was faring. He hoped to visit her this time and to convince her that he had had no alternative but to marry Jean — that "a damning conjuncture of circumstance" had compelled his actions. He advised her of his intended visit to Edinburgh and his desire to see her again but, in no mood for forgiveness, she had declared that she now "looked upon his letters with a smile of contempt" and had hinted spitefully that she was thinking of publishing them, to which he had replied with cool logic:

> I have received both your letters, Madam, and ought and would have answered the first long ago; but on what subject could I write you?

> How can you expect a correspondent should write you when you de-
> clare that you mean to preserve his letters with a view sooner or later
> to expose them on the pillory of derision and the rack of criticism?
> This is gagging me completely as to speaking the sentiments of my
> bosom. . . .

but, to placate her, he enclosed a poem newly composed in her honour. By
now, however, Agnes was in no mood to re-establish relations with him.
She had had enough of "the sentiments of his bosom" in view of his surprising *volte face* and the humiliation and chagrin it had brought her but she
was willing, it seemed, to correspond with him on a strictly formal basis and
to exchange poems with him for mutual advice and criticism.

Having now settled Jean and the children in their new quarters in Dumfries, he applied to his Excise employers for a few days leave of absence and
headed for the capital city. Although he had been primed by Ainslie in
advance that there would be little welcome for him in the Potterrow, he felt
certain that the persuasions that had always won her favours would topple
his bird from her lofty perch. His last letter to her had been inveigling:

> I cannot, will not enter into extenuatory circumstances; else I could
> show you how my precipitate, headlong, unthinking conduct was
> leagued with unlucky events to thrust me out of a possibility of keeping
> the path of rectitude; cursed me by an irreconcilable war between my
> duty and my nearest wishes, to damn me with a choice only of a
> different species of error and misconduct. I dare not trust myself
> further with the subject. . . .

He had also been informed by Ainslie that, urged by her relatives and
intimate friends, she intended to attempt a reconciliation with her husband
in Jamaica for the sake of her small children and he decided to present her
with a "parting" gift — a pair of engraved wine goblets — accompanied
by a poignant farewell poem:

> Ae fond kiss and then we sever;
> Ae farewell, and then for ever!
> Deep in heart-wrung tears I'll pledge thee,
> Warring sighs and groans I'll wage thee. . . .
>
> I'll ne'er blame my partial fancy,
> Nothing could resist my Nancy:
> But to see her was to love her:
> Love but her, and love for ever.
>
> Had we never lov'd sae kindly
> Had we never lov'd sae blindly,
> Never met — or never parted,
> We had ne'er been broken-hearted.
>
> Fare-thee-well, thou first and fairest!
> Fare-thee-well, thou best and dearest!
> Thine be every joy and treasure,
> Peace, enjoyment, love and pleasure. . . .

and although she had deprecated him as a "villain" and accused him of "perfidious treachery," the eloquence of his poem touched her lonely, hungry heart and she had consented to meet him for a last time—"in *Friendship* only."

Back once again in Dumfries — the Clarinda affair laid away forever as "un petit egaremen du coeur during my stay in Edinburgh" (he had told Frances Dunlop), he applied himself enthusiastically to such social diversions as the town offered and allied himself with the rampant political issues with which the thronged taverns buzzed. Imprudently he associated himself openly with the Whig cause when it would have been more judicious had he supported the Tories instead since many of the superior Excise officers were staunch Tories and could only regard his apostasy with a jaundiced eye. And rashly, considering his circumstances, he composed a series of Election Ballads in favour of the Whigs — a matter that did not escape the attention of his superiors in the Excise Service.

Apart from the political themes which now engaged his pen, he composed a number of poems on historical ones — a *Lament for Mary Queen of Scots;* an *Address of Bruce to his Army;* and an *Epistle* to the Dumfries descendant of that gallant Lord Heries who had begged the Queen to spare the life of Bothwell, instigator of her husband's death. He also composed an *Ode for General Washington* which delighted Scottish supporters of the American Revolution among whom he counted himself. He received a flattering letter of approval from the Earl of Buchan who had sent to Washington "a magnificent and truly characteristic present in the shape of a box elegantly mounted with silver and made of wood from the oak tree that had sheltered the doughty Wallace — the Washington of Scotland."

Already the drums of France's revolutionary forces were beating faintly across the English Channel, the echo of their ominous tattoo reverberating from Land's End to John o' Groats. To a fiercely democratic Burns, their voice was that of an outraged downtrodden peasantry raised in revolt against an age-old autocracy. Nationalist at heart and wearing his confessed Jacobitism like a sprig of heather in his bonnet, he deplored the fact that a Hanoverian monarch usurped the Scottish throne now vanished in the mists of time and he began to contribute indiscreet items to newspapers over the *non de plume* "A Friend of the People." He had composed for Johnson's *Musical Museum* a number of songs that deplored the loss of Scotland's jewelled crown and the humiliating servitude of her people. He blasted "the coward few" who had sold out the independence of their country "for hireling traitors' wages" and those who had "sold Scotland for English gold." He wrote passionately to Frances Dunlop: "Alas! have I often said to myself, what are all the advantages which my country reaps from the union of the Crowns that can counterbalance the annihilation of her independence and even her very name. Nothing can reconcile me to the terms *English* ambassador and *English* court." But Frances Dunlop, with male relatives and sons-in-law serving in France's Royalist armies, took a dim view of his rantings and feared they would land him in trouble with his employers who discouraged political utterances on the part of their officers and she warned him that it would be better if he put an extinguisher on his flaming heresies. Some of his other indiscretions worried her too. She had heard that, with more time on his hands in Dumfries, he was constantly frequenting the taverns where men's tongues were loosed and that he had been guilty of composing bawdy ballads for their enjoyment. She had chided him about dangerous looseness and, in a touchy and resentful mood, he replied: "I am very sorry that you should be informed of my supposed guilt in composing in some midnight frolic, a stanza or two perhaps not quite proper for a clergyman's reading to a company of ladies. That I am the author of the verses alluded to in your letter is what I much doubt. You may guess that the convivial hours of *men* have their mysteries of wit and mirth; and I hold it a piece of contemptible baseness to detail the sallies of thoughtless merriment of the orgies of accidental intoxication to the ear of cool Sobriety or female Delicacy . . ."

All too soon, however, the heresies of Mr. Burns were reported to his superiors by those who had good reason to resent his official intrusion into their private sins and in due course he was summoned by the Board of Excise Commissioners to defend his behaviour. Commissioner Mitchell, a high ranking officer in the area, had received from the Commissioners in Edinburgh orders to "enquire into the political conduct of Mr. Burns as a person disaffected to the Government."

Dismayed by agonizing visions of what was likely to happen to his family should he be deprived of his living by his apostasy, and frantic with worry, Robert wrote to his friend Graham of Fintry (of the Excise) beseeching his immediate intercession:

> Sir, you are a husband and a father — you know what you would feel to see the much-loved wife of your bosom and your helpless, prattling little ones turned adrift into the world, degraded and disgraced from a situation in which they had been respectable and respected, and left almost without the necessary support of a miserable existence. Alas, Sir! must I think that such, soon, will be my lot? and from the damned, dark insinuations of hellish, groundless envy, too!

He "would not tell a deliberate falsehood even though worse horrors than dismissal hung over his head," he assured Graham. "The allegation, whatever villain made it, is a lie. To the British Constitution, next after my God, I am most devoutly attached." And he made one last impassioned plea to the kindly Graham:

> You, Sir, have been much and generously my friend. Heaven knows how warmly I have felt the obligation and how gratefully I have thanked you. Fortune, Sir, has made you powerful and me impotent; has given you patronage and me dependence. I would not for my single self call on your humanity; were such my insular situation I

would despise the tear that now wells in my eye — I would brave misfortune; I could face ruin; for, at the worst, 'Death's thousand doors stand open.' But, good God! the tender concerns I have mentioned, the claims and ties that I see at this moment, how they unnerve courage and wither resolution! To your patronage, as a man of some genius, you have allowed me a claim; and your esteem as an honest man I know is my due: to these, Sir, permit me to appeal — to save me from that misery which threatens to overwhelm me and which, with my latest breath I will say, I have not deserved.

He had been accused by his detractors of not only belonging to, but actually heading a disloyal political group; of "uttering invectives against the King" and of refusing to stand up in a local theatre when *God Save the King* had been sung, even if he were so intoxicated as to have been unable to rise. He had also been accused of subscribing to a revolutionary newspaper called the *Edinburgh Gazette* and of contributing himself to its pages. On the latter count, Robert told Graham, his accusers had been completely wide of the mark. The only contribution he had ever made to its pages was a poetic *Address on the Rights of Women* recited by a popular actress on her Benefit Night at an Edinburgh theatre. It had absolutely nothing whatever to do with politics and as for his sympathy for the causes of the French Revolution:

> As for France, I was her enthusiastic votary in the beginning of the business. When she came to show her old avidity for conquest in annexing Savoy, etc. to her dominions and invading the rights of Holland, I altered my sentiments. A tippling ballad which I composed on the prince of Brunswick's breaking up his camp — and sung at one convivial evening — I shall send you also, sealed up, as it is not for everybody's reading. The latter is not worth your perusal but, lest Fame should — as she had already done — use and even abuse her old privilege of lying — you shall be the judge of everything, *le pour et le contre* of my political writings and conduct.

As for vilifying the British monarch, that, too, was a baseless calumny, he told Graham: "I never uttered any invective against the King. His private worth it is impossible that a man like myself can appreciate; but in his public capacity I always revered, and always will, with the soundest loyalty, the monarch of Great Britain as (to speak Masonically) the sacred Keystone of our Royal Arch Constitution."

For all his protestation of innocence, however, some with long memories to animate their long tongues, recalled a previous glaring indiscretion. Once, visiting the castle of Stirling, he had inscribed a treasonable stanza on the window of a local inn — *On Seeing the Royal Palace in Ruins:*

> Here Stuarts once in glory reigned
> And laws for Scotland's weal ordained;
> But now unroof'd their palace stands,
> Their sceptre's sway'd by other hands;
> Fallen, indeed, and to the earth,
> Whence grovelling reptiles take their birth.

> The injur'd Stuart line is gone,
> A race outlandish fills their throne;
> An idiot race, to honour lost;
> Who knows them best despise them most.

The treasonable lines had created a stir and they had been copied and printed in certain newspapers. King George the Third was suffering his first fits of incipient insanity and, consequently, the lines were in shocking bad taste and Burns had been accused of "basely stabbing his monarch's fame while skulking with a villain's aim." At the time he had been a candidate for employment in the Excise, he had been "questioned like a child about my matters and blamed and schooled for my inscription on the Stirling window," he had told Clarinda. At a later date, however, he had re-visited Stirling and had deliberately smashed the telltale window-pane, paying the inn landlord for the damage.

When, not long before, tributes had appeared in Scottish newspapers on the occasion of the British monarch's Birthday, he had composed a poem entitled *A Dream* in which he had imagined himself attending the Birthday *Levee* and presenting a poetic address of his own. He had sent copies of the poem to some of his friends but, in the eyes of Frances Dunlop, Mrs. Stewart of Stair and other socialites, it was perilous stuff and Frances Dunlop begged him to withhold it from the next edition of his *Poems*. This he flatly declined to do, commenting to a friend: "I set as little by princes, lords, clergy, critics, etc. as all these respective gentry do by my bardship . . . Poets much my superior have so flattered those who possessed the adventitious qualities of wealth and power, that I am determined to flatter no created being, either in prose or verse." His gently born female critics were willing to condone certain sentiments expressed in the *Dream* but they boggled at the indelicacy and innuendo in two of its verses referring chiefly to the young Prince of Wales — notorious for his dissolute and extravagant ways — and the dig at a Royal sailor who was engaged in a disreputable *liaison:*

> For you, young potentate of Wales
>   I tell your Highness fairly.
> Down pleasure's stream wi' swelling sails
>   I'm told you're driving rarely;
> But some day ye may gnaw your nails,
>   An' curse your folly sairly
> That e'er ye brak Diana's pales
>   Or rattled dice wi' Charlie
>   By night or day.
> Young royal "Tarry Breeks," I learn
>   Ye've lately come athwart her;
> A glorious galley, stem an' stern,
>   Well-rigged for Venus barter;
> But first hand out, that she'll discern
>   Your hymeneal charter,

> Then heave aboard your grappling iron
> An' large upon her quarter
> Come full that day.

Such suggestive bawdry might be welcome enough in the disreputable taverns thronged by rioting patrons in their cups but it had no place in the circumspect social circles that fringed the august Assembly Rooms of the Court.

The Board of Excise Commissioners took their time in looking into the sins of their newest recruit but after much correspondence back and forth between Dumfries and Edinburgh and favourable pressures from influential quarters, it was decided that Poet Burns was not to be judged by ordinary standards: nevertheless, he was to be advised in no uncertain terms that in future it would be his duty "to *act,* not to *think,*" and that when provocation arose he was to be "silent and obedient." It was for others to tip their arrows at Whitehall and to advocate parliamentary reform. No Government employee — much less an Exciseman — could be guilty of such heresy if he knew on which side his bread was buttered.

Robert breathed a sigh of prodigious relief. His sins had been obviously forgiven him and he determined to try to justify his Excise superior's confidential assessment of him in official records: "Robert Burns, a Poet, turns out well," though he deplored to intimate friends "the hate of those who watched for his halting and the contumelious sneer of those whom accident had made his superiors." However, "to rail against the prejudices which had been raised against him was not the purpose of his letters," he assured them. Indeed, he wrote, "it is a warfare I know not how to wage. The powers of vice I can in some degree calculate, and against direct malevolence I can be on my guard; but who can estimate the fatuity of giddy caprice or ward off the unthinking mischief of precipitate folly?" The sweet wine of victory was soured by the bitterness he felt in his heart towards his enemies but there was consolation in the thought that he was not the first man — nor would he be the last — to discover that bread earned in the service of exacting employers was likely to prove indigestible for those of independent thinking.

News of his troubles had travelled far afield and it had been rumored in Ayrshire and in Edinburgh that he had been actually dismissed from the Service. Generous friends, headed by John Francis Erskine (afterwards Earl of Marr) had promptly opened a subscription fund for his benefit. The rumours had also reached the ears of Frances Dunlop who, truth to tell, had long been expecting such a disastrous turn of events. She sent him a line of sympathy to which he replied at some length, defending one by one the charges that had been brought against him and to Erskine who had started the benefit fund he explained that things were not as bad as they seemed:

> You have been misinformed as to my final dismissal from the Excise: I
> am still in the Service. Indeed, but for the exertions of a gentleman who
> must be known to you, Mr. Graham of Fintry — a gentleman who has

been my warm and generous friend — I had, without so much as a hearing or the smallest previous intimation, been turned adrift with my helpless family, to all the horrors of want. Had I any other resources probably I might have saved them the trouble of a dismissal. Mr. Corbet (Supervisor-General of the Excise) was likewise my steady friend, so between Graham and him, I have been partly forgiven. . . .

He feared, however, that his reckless indiscretions might have cost him the promotion to a supervisorship he had been ardently angling for, he told Erskine. He had probably paid dearly for his mad patriotic fervours and his liquor-loosened tongue.

He confided little of his Excise troubles and apprehensions to Jean for their tiny daughter, Elizabeth Riddel, was ailing and fretful and they despaired of rearing her. He did not want to add to Jean's multiple domestic cares and he bore his Excise miseries in silence, hoping that his employers would prove to be men of charity and tolerance.

Jean was anxious to have baby Bess brought from Mossgiel to join the little household in Dumfries and since Jean would undoubtedly bear more children in the years to come, Robert looked around for a new dwelling and was successful in finding a more commodious self-contained house in the Mill Vennel. With its comfortable ground-floor parlour and kitchen, two bedrooms above and an attic for the children to sleep in, it was a vast improvement on their cramped quarters in the Stinking Vennel. Its annual rent was a modest £8 and it was the kind of residence usually occupied by the better-class townsfolk. The move took place on the 10th of May and, adding to Robert's new feeling of well-being, he received in the following month a copy of Thomson's *Select Collection* which contained many of his own contributions.

CHAPTER 11

The ice barrier that had separated Robert and Agnes McLehose had been partially thawed by their contact during his last visit to Edinburgh and his propitiatory gift of the drinking goblets and the poetic tribute which accompanied them.

She had returned from the West Indies after a disillusioning brief reunion with her husband upset by the discovery that he was now saddled with a mulatto family and that, in spite of his promises to reform and his improved financial situation, he was still short-tempered, inconsiderate and shiftless. Explaining to friends that the Jamaican climate had not suited her, she had returned to Scotland on the ship that had taken her out and, lonely and disconsolate, she had delayed sending the news to Robert. She had lost many of her former Edinburgh friends on account of her clandestine liaison with him and, while glad of the prospect of renewed association with him as an antidote for loneliness, she insisted that renewed correspondence between them must be "in Friendship only." He agreed to her terms but pleaded: "I have many a time taken up my pen to try an epistle of "Friendship" to you; but it will not do. 'Tis like Jove grasping a pop-gun after having wielded his thunder! When I take up my pen, recollection ruins me. Ah! my ever-dearest Clarinda! What a host of Memory's tenderest offspring crowd round my fancy at that name! But I must not indulge that subject; you have forbid it . . ."

Still paying poetic tribute to Jean's charms, he concentrated now on his contributions to the works of Johnson and Thomson, polishing up some long-extant poems on the subject of matrimonial bondage which gave rise to speculative conjecture that they probably reflected discord on the author's own home front and that Burns was beginning to strain at the connubial leash. Jean rebutted these rumours with amused tolerance and went serenely on her way, solacing the noisy fretful children, preparing for the next pregnancy, placating Robert during what he called his "blue devil hours" and devising ways and means to stretch the family budget.

In tribute to his fame, Robert had been made an honorary Burgess of the Town of Dumfries and had applied to its Lord Provost, Bailies and Town Council for the privilege of free education for his sons, claiming that his small Excise income "bore hard on him" and that the town of Dumfries had been made richer by the sum of £10 derived from fines levied by himself on 200 barrels of ale — a source of income that had been overlooked by his predecessors. Robert junior — lone survvior of Jean's first twins — was now nine years old and showing marked ability scholastically under his father's spare time tutoring. The request was granted, easing the family budget at a somewhat difficult time.

Once again, however, Robert in his cups had been foolhardy enough to air his political views at the dinner table of a prominent host. He had proposed a toast that lauded the virtues of George Washington at the expense of a British leader and the toast had been loudly objected to by a naval officer present. Ugly words had flared between them. Dreading the consequences of his rashness, Robert wrote an influential friend the next day begging for his immediate intervention. "I know I was drunk last night, but I am sober this morning," he confessed. "The toast I proposed was one that could not possibly be objected to by reasonable people. The words uttered between us were such as generally end in a brace of pistols, but I am pleased to think that I did not ruin the peace and welfare of a wife and family in a drunken squabble," and he explained: "The report of certain political opinions being mine had already once before brought me to the brink of destruction and I dreaded last night's business might be misinterpreted in the same way." But once again — his stars being in favourable aspect — he was forgiven by his superiors who were inclined to agree that Mr. Burns, fortified by spirits, was understandably prone to commit plebeian illbred *gaffes*. And, anxious to demonstrate where his true loyalties lay, Robert joined the recruiting Dumfries Volunteers and when rumours circulated that France intended to invade England, he composed a spirited ballad entitled *Does Haughty Gaul Invasion Threat?* calculated to convince his detractors that he was really at heart a loyal King's man.

Although his enthusiasm for Thomson's *Collection of Songs* was in no way diminished, he found the publisher a somewhat demanding critic who sometimes objected to the verses and sometimes to the airs he was supplying and he wrote: "Making a poem is like begetting a son: you cannot know whether you have a wise man or a fool until you produce him to the world and try him. For that reason I send you the offspring of my brain, *abortions* and all; and, as such, pray look over them and forgive them and burn them." He defended some of his least-appealing performances on the grounds that some of the airs to which he married his original verses had once been Romish liturgical chants and that, during the Reformation, reformers had burlesqued some of the old tunes and set bawdy verses to them; but that, surprisingly enough, the verses actually seemed to fit the music. An expedient merchandiser, Thomson also suggested that, in order to increase the market for his wares, he should try his hand at English verses but to these persuasions he had turned a deaf ear, declaring hotly "These English songs gravel me to death; I have not that command of the language that I have of my native tongue," but he agreed to experiment a little in that direction.

At the end of July when the heat in Dumfries became oppressive, Robert set out on a tour of Galloway in the company of a congenial friend named Syme who had occupied the ground floor of his former residence in the Stinking Vennel. He hoped for new inspiration and tempting themes for his pen and Galloway teemed with historical associations. Only recently Louis XVI of France had been executed and the populace had demanded the head of his consort, the Austrian Marie Antoinette. These multiplying horrors lay heavily on his spirits. A tour of the Scottish countryside, besides furnishing fresh themes for his pen would serve to dispel them from his mind for a time.

Early the following year another son was born to Robert and Jean and he was named James Glencairn in memory of Robert's former patron who, after vainly seeking health abroad in Spain, had returned to Scotland to die at Falmouth as his ship touched port. Deeply moved by the Earl's death, Robert had composed a *Lament* which he sent to Lady Cunningham, the Earl's sister, declaring: "If amongst my children I shall have a son that has a heart, he shall hand the name to his child as a family honour and a family debt, that my dearest existence I owe to the noble house of Glencairn" and to Frances Dunlop he had written: "I shall make all my children's names altars of gratitude. Poor, dear little souls, they are all the finest creatures in the world. I gratefully thank my God for his goodness in that respect. A fine constitution and amiable dispositions are of immense consequence to the happiness of the individual." And he gave full credit to Jean for the heritage of robust health and amiability she had passed on to her small sons. Laughingly he had reminded her one day that she was fit to be the mother of a regiment and, with the complacency he had come to adore, she had merrily pointed out that there was still room on the blank pages of their family bible for a few more names.

His own health was becoming increasingly precarious, his temper more irritable and Jean noted with dismay that the old buoyancy had gone out of his step. Depression and physical fatigue was driving him more often to the local tavern and he was eager to accept invitations of socialite hosts that now poured in upon him. His well-heeled hosts, however, were able to sleep off their excesses the following day, while Robert was compelled to be up and about early in the performance of his duties. Detractors, envious of his popularity and success, circulated calumnies against him but warm friends and admirers sprang to his defence, their hearts touched by his obvious physical decline and low spirits. A sympathetic observer later on wrote, "In the intervals between his occasions of intemperance brought on by the excesses of the day, he suffered the keenest anguish of remorse. His

102

Jean behaved with a degree of maternal and conjugal tenderness and prudence that made him feel more bitterly the evils of his conduct." Wrote another: "His aberrations were occasional, not systematic, and they were, to himself, a source of great misery in retrospect but in spite of his transient follies, he never ceased to be an affectionate father and husband; and if Jean had her own particular causes for dissatisfaction, she never showed it. She knew they were the aberrations of a man who encountered more temptation from without and within that the immense majority of mankind who, far from having to contend against, are even able to imagine."

Shortly after the birth of little James Glencairn, Robert was appointed Acting Supervisor during the illness of his superior, an indulgence that went far to spark the flame of his flagging spirits and he carried out his new duties and responsibilities with great credit.

Frequently assailed now by bouts of rheumatism aggravated by constant exposure to inclement weather and by overheating with wine and spirituous liquors at the tables of his hosts, he began to ignore the personal correspondence that had once meant so much to him. At the end of the year, apologizing to Frances Dunlop for his long silence, he conveyed news of the death of his favourite child — tiny two and a half year old Elizabeth Riddel — an event that had almost prostrated him. Far afield on his Excise duties at the time, he had been unable to attend the child's funeral in Mauchline. More and more his thoughts toyed with the theme of death and he worried constantly about the future of his family should he be taken away from them soon. "I cannot describe to you the anxious, sleepless hours my family ties have given me," he wrote Frances Dunlop. "I see a train of helpless little folk; me and my exertions all their stay. On what a brittle thread does the life of man hang! If I am to be nipt off at the command of fate, even in all the vigour of manhood — and such things happen every day — Gracious God! what would become of my little flock! 'Tis here I envy you people of fortune . . . able to leave your loved ones independence and friends; while I — but I shall become distracted if I pursue this subject further . . ."

To others he complained that the prevailing war between England and France was depriving him of part of his income which came from fines levied on smuggled imports now proscribed; that he often suffered violent attacks of toothache — "fifty troops of infernal spirits driving from ear to ear along his jawbones" — and that he was so short of ready cash that he might have to borrow from friends to pay his modest rent. "Scarcely had I begun to recover from the loss of my only daughter and darling child, when I myself became a victim of rheumatic fever which brought me to the borders of the grave," he wrote to a distant friend. "Long the die spun doubtful; until after many weeks of a sick-bed, it seems to have turned up life and I am beginning to crawl across my room and have been once before my own door in the street." Unfamiliar with the real nature of his disease (today classified as rheumatic endocarditis, a disease of the lining of the heart) his doctors recommended salt sea bathing at a hamlet called Brow on the Solway Firth nine miles from Dumfries. Here, it was hoped, the saline waters of the Brow well, left by retreating tides, might gradually allay his rheumatic tortures. In the light of subsequent medical knowledge, however, it might seem that bodily immersion in the chilly waters of the Brow well was almost suicidal for what his doctors classified as a "flying gout."

Wracked with anxiety about the situation of his family if he were placed on half-pay due to absence from his Excise duties, he wrote a friend asking him to use his influence with the Board of Commissioners in his behalf: "What way, in the name of thrift, shall I maintain myself and keep a horse in these country quarters, with a wife and children at home, on £35?" he implored. "If they do not grant me full salary, I must exit *en poet;* if I do not die of disease, I must perish with hunger." But thanks to the kindness of Graham of Fintry who promptly collected some funds for the family's immediate relief and thanks to the friendly young Excise employee who undertook to shoulder Burns's duties during his absence, his tormenting anxieties were momentarily allayed. The much-vaunted remedial virtues of the Brow well brought him little relief, however, and he wrote dejectedly to Gilbert at Mossgiel:

> It will be no very pleasing news to you to be told that I am dangerously ill and not likely to get better. An inveterate rheumatism has reduced me to such a state of debility and my appetite is so totally gone that I can scarcely stand on my legs. I have been a week at sea bathing and I will continue there or at a friend's house in the country all summer. God keep my wife and children; if I am taken from their head they will be poor indeed. I have contracted one or two serious debts, partly from my illness and party from too much thoughtlessness as to expense when I came to Dumfries, that it will cut in too much on the little I leave in your hands. . . .

This was the sum of the interest-bearing £180 he had loaned Gilbert to see him through his emergencies at Mossgiel. He did not want to alarm Jean unduly for she was once more in the family way and her time was getting short but he wrote her:

> My Dearest Love,
> I delayed writing until I could tell you what effect sea bathing was likely to produce. It would be injustice to deny that it has eased my pains and I think it has strengthened me; but my appetite is still extremely bad. No flesh nor fish can I swallow; porridge and milk are the only things I can taste. . . .

The lamp was burning dangerously low and he knew it and because the plight of Jean, soon to face her confinement alone without the consolation of his nearness, distracted him, he penned a hasty line to James Armour begging for the help of her mother who was then visiting in Fife:

> For Heaven's sake, as you value the welfare of your daughter and my wife, do, my dearest Sir, write to Fife to Mrs. Armour to come if pos-

sible. The medical men have ordered me, *as I value my existence,* to fly to sea bathing and country quarters; so it is ten thousand chances to one that I shall not be within a dozen miles of her when her hour comes. What a situation for her to be in, poor girl, without a single friend near her at such a serious moment! I have been a week at salt water and though I think I have got some good by it, I have secret fears that this business will be dangerous if not fatal. . . .

and, all bitterness and rancour past, he signed his letter "Your affectionate son."

He had few illusions about the possibility of early recovery and he wrote Frances Dunlop that his disease was likely to send him to *"that bourne from whence no traveller returns,"* underlining the words for emphasis. He also wrote to a distant schoolmaster friend who had always been sympathetic: "Alas, Clarke! I begin to fear the worst. As to my individual self, I am tranquil and would despise myself if I were not; but Burns's widow and half a dozen of his dear little ones— helpless orphans — there I am weak as a woman's tear. If I must go, I shall leave a few friends behind me whom I shall regret while consciousness remains. That I shall see you again is, I'm afraid, highly improbable."

Weak, emaciated and feverish, he left Brow on the 18th of July, returning to Dumfries in a gig borrowed from a friend and when he dismounted from the vehicle at his own front door he was unable to stand and Jean, waiting to welcome him with outstretched arms, was struck dumb with secret terror at his pitiful appearance. Unable to mount the stairs to the room that had been prepared for him, he was guided to a makeshift bed in a room on the ground floor. The children had been sent to the home of a neighbour and young Jessie Lewars, sister of the Excise employee who had kindly assumed Robert's duties during his illness, came in to help Jean at the critical hour. No reply had been received in answer to his distracted letter to James Armour and, rousing himself from his torpor with a supreme effort, he mustered enough strength to pen another line:

> Do, for Heaven's sake, send Mrs. Armour here immediately. My wife is hourly expecting to be put to bed. Good God! What a situation for her to be in, poor girl, without a friend. I returned from sea bathing quarters today and my medical friends would almost persuade me that I am better; but I think and feel that my strength is so gone that the disorder will prove fatal to me.

They were percipient and truly prophetic words. He lingered listlessly for two more days, haunted by crucifying fears that he would be thrown into jail for money he owed a Dumfries tailor who, convinced that he was about to die, had dunned him for payment for his Dumfries Volunteers uniform. On the third day his small children were brought home for a last look at their celebrated father and, unconscious of their presence, he passed away, his troubled spirit released from earthly pressures.

Those who came to see him as he lay in death were deeply moved by the serenity of his countenance. "He lay in a plain unadorned coffin with a linen sheet drawn over his face and on the bed and around his body herbs and flowers were thickly strewn," related a commentator. "He was wasted by long illness but death had not increased the swarthy hue of his face which was uncommonly dark and deeply marked. His broad and open brow was pale and serene and around it his sable hair lay in masses, slightly touched with gray. The room where he lay was plain and neat and the simplicity of his humble dwelling pressed the presence of death more closely on the heart than if his bier had been embellished and blazoned with the trappings of high ancestry or rank." Wrote another reporter later: "As he lay stretched, his dark hair already streaked with unnatural gray, all unworthiness fell away from him . . . and left pure nobleness. Farmer no longer, subject no longer to criticism, to misrepresentation, to the malevolence of mean natures and evil tongues, he lay there, the great Poet of his country, dead too early for himself and for it. He had passed from the judgments of Dumfries and had made his appeal to time." Once, in a moment of introspection, he had told Jean laughingly: "Don't worry, lass, I'll be much more respected a hundred years from now," and he had written an intimate friend: "When I am laid in my grave I wish to be stretched at my full length that I may occupy every inch that I have a right to." He was buried in a simple grave in the southwest corner of St. Michael's churchyard and, paying eloquent tribute to his genius, a commentator wrote: "Of everything the poet was brimful and overflowing. He had his errors but they arose out of his splendid and perilous richness. It is difficult to carry a full cup and not spill it."

A vast assembly of twelve thousand townsfolk and distinguished "incomers" followed his cortege to the churchyard and at the graveside his old companions of the Dumfries Volunteers fired three ragged volleys that served not only as a *requiem* for Robert Burns but also as a *feu de joie* marking the birth of his son born to Jean during the funeral services and named Maxwell after the doctor who had attended Robert during his last days on earth; a child that soon followed his father to the grave.

Alexander Cunningham, an intimate friend of the family, wrote a poignant description of Jean and her children as they emerged soon after the funeral from the house in the Mill-hole Brae:

> . . . a weeping widow and four helpless sons; they came into the streets in their mourning clothes and public sympathy was awakened afresh. I shall never forget the look of his boys and the compassion they excited. The poet's life had not been without errors, and such errors, too, as a wife is slow in forgiving; but he was honoured then and he is honoured now by the unalienable affection of his wife; and the world repays her prudence and love by its regard and esteem. . . .

Realistic and practical-minded to a degree and seldom given to flights of metaphysical fancy, Jean Armour Burns later confided to a friend that not long after his death Robert, a *revenant,* had appeared one night at her bedside "gazing intently and with a great love at the child sleeping in her arms" — the tiny babe he had never seen. The vision brought immeasurable comfort to the mourning Jean. It seemed like a portent from Beyond the Veil that her long loved Robert watched over his little flock and that all would be well with them.

Not yet thirty years of age when her husband died — and still a handsome and fascinating woman according to her contemporaries, Jean Armour Burns received several offers of marriage, two of which would have established her comfortably financially but she preferred to live out the rest of her days as the widow of Robert Burns and the mother of his sons.

The only income she possessed at Robert's death was a tiny annuity of £10 derived from a Benefit Society connected with the Excise but a public subscription was opened in her behalf which soon amounted to £700 and, in addition, a new edition of her late husband's works, edited by Dr. Currie, brought in the handsome sum of £2000. With this assistance, augmented by Parliament and a benevolent Lord Panmure in the matter of a small annuity of £50, she was able to live on comfortably in the house in which Robert had died and to educate her young sons until they were able to make their own way in the world.

Robert, the eldest boy, attended university for three sessions later on and subsequently obtained a government position in the Stamp Office in London where he served for some thirty years. Francis Wallace, regarded as the most promising of all Robert's sons, died at the age of fourteen and was buried beside his father. At the age of fifteen, William Nichol enlisted as a midshipman on an East India ship, was promoted to a cadetship and served later in the Indian Army. Maxwell, the child born on the day of his father's funeral, lived only three short years and was also buried beside his illustrious father; while James Glencairn, the most robust of Jean's sons, served first as a cadet in the service of the East India Company, was later commissioned in rank and went on to a long and distinguished career in India.

There were some who considered that the legitimate children of Burns were not the only offspring entitled to public support and Alderman Shaw of London, a former Ayrshireman, promoted a fund of £400 to be divided equally between Lizzie Paton's "sonsie, smirkin' dear-bought Bess" and the child of Ann Park, niece of the Hyslops, proprietors of the Globe Inn in Dumfries. Jean was delighted by this provision for Robert's natural children and kept closely in touch with the two girls in the years that lay ahead. Half the fund was to be paid to each girl when she reached the age of twenty-one or when she married and if either of them died before the endowment fell due, her share was to pass to the other. Both girls subsequently married and passed obscurely into history.

Jean lived on modestly and circumspectly in the house in which Robert had died and, after thirty-eight years of widowhood, she died at the age of sixty-seven. The *Dumfries Courier* reported her demise as follows:

> At a late hour on the night of Wednesday, the 26th of March, the world and its concerns closed forever on Mrs. Jean Armour Burns — the venerable relict of the poet Burns.
>
> On the Saturday preceding, she was seized with paralysis for the fourth time during the last few years and, although perfectly conscious of her situation and the presence of friends, she became deprived, before being removed to bed, of the faculty of speech and in a day or two thereafter of the sense of hearing. Still, she lay wonderfully calm and composed and, in the opinion of her medical attendants, suffered from weakness rather than pain.
>
> On the night of Tuesday or morning of Wednesday, a fifth stroke, unperceived by her attendants, deprived Mrs. Burns of mental consciousness and from that time till the hour of her death her situation was that of a breathing corpse. And thus passed away all that remained of Burns's Bonnie Jean.

On the first day of April, 1834 — almost half a century from the April day when she had first met Robert Burns on the Mauchline bleaching-green — the body of Jean Armour Burns was borne to the Mausoleum which contained his remains that had been previously transferred from his first obscure grave in St. Michael's churchyard. An immense throng of Dumfries townsfolk accompanied her body to its place beside her famous husband for, during her long residence in Dumfries, she had won the respect and admiration of all who knew her.

The papers were eagerly scanned for particulars of her intimate association with Burns and Editor McDiarmid of the *Courier* declared: "When young, she must have been a handsome, comely woman, if not indeed a beauty, when the poet saw her for the first time on a Mauchline bleach-green. Her limbs were cast in the finest mould and up to middle life her jet black eyes were clear and sparkling, her deportment easy and her step light. She moved with great grace on the floor and sang in a style but rarely equalled by unprofessional singers. Her memory, too, was strong and she could quote at great length and with much aptitude. Of these powers the Bard was so well aware that he read to her almost every piece he composed and was not ashamed to own that he had profited by her judgment. After the death of Burns she was visited by thousands of strangers from the peer to itinerant sonneteers — a class of persons to whom she never refused an audience or dismissed unrewarded. Occasionally, during the summer months, she was a good deal annoyed; but she bore all these invasions in patience and, although naturally fond of quiet, seemed to consider her house open to visitors and its mistress, to some degree, the property of the public. Hers was one of those well-balanced minds that cling instinctively to propriety and a medium in all things; and such as knew the deceased, early and late, were unconscious of any change in her demeanour and habits excepting, perhaps, greater attention to dress and more refinement of manner, unconsciously acquired by frequent association with families of the first respectability. In her tastes she was frugal, simple and pure; and delighted in music, pictures and flowers. In the spring and summer it was impossible to pass her windows without being impressed by the floral treasures they contained; and if extravagant in anything, it was in the purchase of roots and flowers and plants of the finest sorts. Fond of the society of young people, she mingled as long as she could in their innocent pleasures and cheerfully filled for them the cup that cheers but not inebriates. She was a clever woman, possessed of great shrewdness, discriminated character admirably and frequently made very pithy remarks . . ." and he declared that, after her son Captain James Glencairn had enabled her to relinquish the small charitable pensions awarded her by sympathetic friends, she enjoyed an income of about two hundred pounds a year "a great part of which, as not needed by her, she dispensed in charities."

The wedding ring she wore as the wife and widow of Burns — a comparatively large slender gold band, worn thin by the passage of the years — is now to be seen in the museum of the Burns Monument at Alloway which also contains the bibles the poet once gave to Highland Mary and the engraved goblets he had presented to Clarinda. In the final analysis, however, the wedding ring of Jean Armour Burns is an eloquent witness to her place in the mutable affections of Burns. She, perhaps more than any other woman he had ever loved, understood what he meant when, less than two years before his death, he had written to his publisher Thomson: "I am sensible, my dear friend, that a genuine poet can no more exist without his mistress than his meat" and — in a subsequent letter — "Conjugal love is a passion which I deeply feel and highly venerate; but somehow it does not make such a figure in poesy as that other species of the passion. Where Love is liberty and Nature law. Musically speaking, the first is an instrument of which the gamut is scanty and confined, but the tones inexpressibly sweet; while the last has powers equal to all the intellectual modulations of the human soul." And, wishing apparently to elaborate the theme more explicitly, he had added: "Still, I am a very poet in my enthusiasm of the passion. The welfare and happiness of the beloved object is the first and inviolate sentiment that pervades my soul; and whatever pleasures I might wish for, or whatever might be the raptures they would give me, yet if they interfere with that first principle, it is having these pleasures at a dishonest price; and justice forbids, and generosity disdains the purchase. As to the herd of the sex who are good for little or nothing else, however, I have made no such agreement with myself; but where the parties are capable of, and the passion is the true Divinity of Love — a man who can act otherwise is a villain!" It was a candid confession and perhaps a cynical one.

Writing to an intimate friend after the death of Bonnie Jean, Betty Burns, the poet's illegitimate daughter by Ann Park of the Globe Inn, Dumfries, declared: "There was something good and charitable about her surpassing all women I ever yet met with."

In Jean Armour he had met an infinitely tolerant and understanding mate and one who had herself known what it was to be carried away by the strong and treacherous tides of the illicit raptures he had, from time to time, found irresistible. And for her percipience and magnificent forbearance he had adored her.

BIBLIOGRAPHY

Primary Sources

Life of the Poet, J. G. Lockhart, prefacing The Works of Robert Burn in 5 vols. (Blackie & Son Limited, London, Glasgow, Edinburgh and Dublin) 1887

Essays on life of Burns by Thomas Carlyle and Professor Wilson edited by Charles Annandale, M.A., LL.D. (same edition)

Memoirs on Life and Works of Robert Burns by George Gilfillan, Hately Waddell and W. Scott Douglas.

"Original Memoir of the Late Robert Burns," Heron, Edin. 1797

Life and Works of Burns, Currie, Edin. 1800

Life of Burns, Josiah Walker, Edin. 1811

Life of Burns, Alexander Peterkin, Edin. 1813

Life of Burns, Rev. Hamilton Paul, Ayr, 1819

Life of Robert Burns, John Gibson Lockhart, Edin. 1830

Life of Burns, Alexander Cunningham, Edin. 1834

Life and Works of Burns, Robert Chambers, Edin. 1851

Life of Burns in "National Burns," Rev. George Gilfillan, 1878

Biographical Memoir for Globe Edition of Poet's Works, Alexander Smith, Edin. 1868

Robert Burns (English Men of Letters), Principal Shairp of St. Andrew's, 1879

Life of Burns, a Spiritual Biography, Dr. Hately Waddell, Edin. 1867

The Land of Burns (Steel Engravings by D. O. Hill), Blackie and Son Limited, Edin. 1837

Complete Poetical and Prose Works of Robert Burns with Life, Notes and Correspondence, Alexander Cunningham, Leavitt & Allen, New York

Secondary Sources

The Letters of Robert Burns, edited by Prof. J. DeLancey Ferguson, Oxford Clarendon Press, 1931

There Was a Lad, Hilton Brown, London, Hamilton, 1949

The Life of Robert Burns, Catherine Carswell, Chatto & Windus, London, 1951

Robert Burns, David Daiches, Rinehart, New York, 1950

Pride and Passion, Prof. J. DeLancey Ferguson, Oxford University Press, 1939

Robert Burns, the Man and His Work, Hans Hecht, translated by Jane Lymburn, Hodge, Edin., 1950

The Russet Coat, Christine Keith, Hale, London, 1956

The Rantin' Dog, John St. Clair Muriel, Liveright, New York, 1947

Man Robert Burns, Grant F. Smith, Ryerson, Toronto

Novels of James Barke, Collins, London, 1959

The Land of Burns, Taylor Gibb, Mauchline

Not Proven, John Gray Wilson, Secker & Warburg, 1960

Life of Robert Burns, Dr. Franklyn Bliss Snyder, Macmillan, New York, 1932

Robert Burns — the Man — His Work — the Legend, Maurice Lindsay, Macgibbon & Kee, London, 1954

The Burns Country, McVie & Shillabeer, Oliver & Boyd, Edinburgh and London, 1962

AUTHOR'S DESCENT:

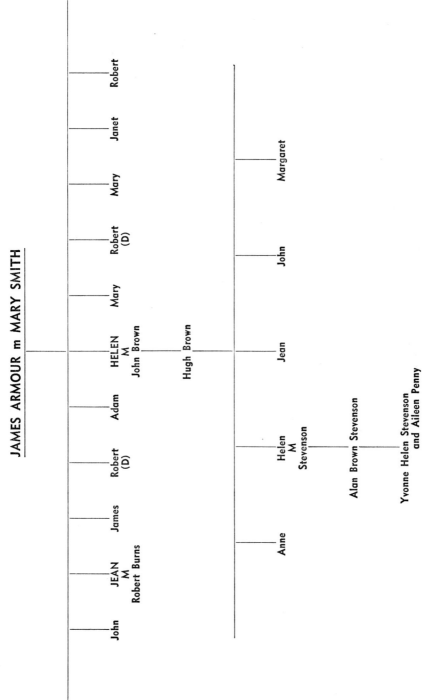

JAMES ARMOUR m MARY SMITH

John | JEAN M Robert Burns | James | Robert (D) | Adam | HELEN M John Brown | Mary | Robert (D) | Mary | Janet | Robert

Hugh Brown

Anne | Helen M Stevenson | Jean | John | Margaret

Alan Brown Stevenson

Yvonne Helen Stevenson and Aileen Penny